MARY BERRY

QUEEN OF BRITISH BAKING

MARY BERRY

QUEEN OF BRITISH BAKING

THE BIOGRAPHY

A S DAGNELL

metro

Published by Metro Publishing
an imprint of John Blake Publishing Ltd
3 Bramber Court, 2 Bramber Road,
London W14 9PB, England

www.johnblakepublishing.co.uk

www.facebook.com/Johnblakepub **facebook**
twitter.com/johnblakepub **twitter**

First published in hardback in 2013
This edition published in 2013

ISBN: 978 1 78219 475 0

British Library Cataloguing-in-Publication Data:

A catalogue record for this book is available from the British Library.

Design by www.envydesign.co.uk

Printed and bound in Great Britain by CPI Group (UK) Ltd

1 3 5 7 9 10 8 6 4 2

Papers used by John Blake Publishing are natural, recyclable products
made from wood grown in sustainable forests. The manufacturing processes
conform to the environmental regulations of the country of origin.

Every attempt has been made to contact the relevant copyright-holders,
but some were unobtainable. We would be grateful if the appropriate people
could contact us.

For Mum, Dad and Nicole

ACKNOWLEDGEMENTS

SOURCES

I have drawn on various newspaper articles from the last 30 years as part of my research for this book. The following newspapers and their supplements have been particularly helpful: *Daily Mirror, Sunday Mirror, Daily Mail, Mail on Sunday, Daily Telegraph, Sunday Telegraph, Daily Express, Sunday Express, Financial Times, Independent, Independent on Sunday, The Times, Sunday Times, Guardian, New York Times, Scotsman, Bath Chronicle, Western Morning News, Gloucestershire Echo, Bucks Free Press Broadcast, Kent Messenger, London Evening Standard, The Journal, Leicester Mercury, Press Association, Brentwood Gazette, Essex Chronicle* and *The Grocer*.

On top of that I have drawn from Mary's appearance on BBC Radio 4's *Desert Island Discs* in 2012 as well as various interviews published on different parts of the BBC's various websites on a number of occasions. Her interviews with ITV News were also very helpful. Her appearances on *Great*

British Bake Off have, of course, been a rich source of information and anecdotes, particularly in writing the latter chapters of this book.

A number of other websites and blogs have been useful sources of information in building a picture of Mary's colourful and exciting life. These include her own website MaryBerry.co.uk, TVCream.co.uk, Wikipedia, YouTube, the websites of the Child Bereavement UK and National Osteoporosis UK charities, the AGA company's official website, The World According To Lady Gaga blog and the hilarious Mary Berry Biting Into Things blog, as well as various BBC websites and the World of Books blog.

THANKS

Special thanks have to go to Kat Lay, a brilliant journalist and friend who helped me with the extensive research of this book. She helped me by ploughing through the newspaper archives, transcribing interviews with Mary and digging out as much information on Mary as she could find. Thanks Kat, I couldn't have done it without you.

Many thanks go to Clive Hebard, who has edited this book. Your guidance, experience and insight have been invaluable and I couldn't have done it without your help.

Also thanks to all my friends who have given me support while writing the biography. In particular Matt Sandy, Donna Bowater, Emma Barrow, Tom McTague, Sian Cox-Brooker, Jonathan Theodore, Sofia de Speluzzi, Martin Brown, Halina Watts, Dan Wootton, Matt Thomas, Sian Grieve, Claire Rees, Lorna Prichard, Ben Glaze, Mandy Lau, Jane Barrow, Sarah Arnold and Jill Main.

Huge thanks also to everyone at the Sunday Mirror for

ACKNOWLEDGEMENTS

their words of wisdom and advice while I was writing. My bosses Caroline Waterston and Claire O'Boyle, thanks for being patient and helping me out. Also Alison Phillips, Gary Jones, Deirdre O'Brien, Ben Griffiths, Justin Penrose, Will Payne, Dean Piper, Hannah Hope, Dominic Herbert, Francesca Cookney, Sarah Turner, Marjorie Yue, Zena Alli, Justine Naylan and Jolene Dearsley.

And most of all thanks to Dad, Mum and my sister Nicole for all the extra help and support as well. Thanks for putting up with me.

CONTENTS

CHAPTER 1

MARY'S STAR RISES

As Mary Berry took a bite out of Janet Basu's croissant, you could have cut the atmosphere with a knife. Four contestants were vying for a place in the prestigious final of one of the year's biggest reality TV shows – and everything was to play for. The winner would have the honour of being crowned the greatest amateur baker in Britain, and this would open up endless possibilities for them. The previous winner of the show had secured a baking book deal, the chance to tour the country showing off their skills, and even the opportunity to develop their own line of baked goods. The contestants knew the possibility of taking their love of baking to the next level was within their grasp. The pressure was on, with an audience of millions watching the contestants' every move with baited breath, anticipating which one of the four would falter at the last hurdle and who would make it through. Loyal fans of the series also knew to watch the judges closely, too, as it all came down to Mary's

1

verdict – what she thought of the buttered, savoury treat that the former French teacher had baked for her. The nervousness on Janet's face was plain to see. Was the croissant too crumbly? Had the heat from the studio lights affected the end result? Was the texture of the pastry right? Or had she used too much butter?

The suspense was such that it would have been easy to imagine that this was the climax of a singing competition like ITV1's *The X Factor* or even BBC1's long-running ballroom dance show *Strictly Come Dancing*. But in fact this was the *Great British Bake Off*, the BBC2 cookery show that was in its second series and heading towards the final. And just like *Britain's Got Talent* and *Strictly*, competition and high drama fuelled the show, only with the carefully rehearsed songs and meticulously choreographed dance routines replaced ... by baked goods.

A surprise hit, the show had blossomed in the year following its first series. Viewing figures had risen from a respectable 2.2 million to in excess of 5 million – a considerable feat for any TV cookery show. After first airing in August 2010, it was safe to say the show had become a veritable triumph, a runaway success; it had become much more popular than its producers could have hoped. No one, not even the creators of the show, could have predicted that so many people would become hooked on a competition revolving around the humble art of baking.

But hooked they were. The ingredients of the show's success were very simple. After a rigorous selection process, a total of 12 home bakers started out at the beginning of each series. They then went head to head against one another, battling it out to be handed the coveted title of

Britain's best baker at the end. Week after week they were put through their paces, as they were given three classic British baked products to impress the judges with. Everything from profiteroles to pork pies was produced in vintage-style village marquees, with the challenges becoming increasingly difficult as the series progressed.

To make the competition as tough as possible, each week the contestants would have to produce three bakes. First they had to cook up a signature bake, to show off their tried-and-tested hand-cooked treats. Next came the technical bake, during which every baker cooked from the same recipe – turning the kitchen into a level playing field but pushing many contestants out of their comfort zone. Then finally the contestants were really put to the test with a show-stopper, allowing them to show off their individual flair and creativity as they produced elaborate creations that really played to their strengths and tested the depth of their individual skills.

On top of the cooking, to add an extra dimension to the show, it was decided that the programme would trace the rich history of British baking by having each episode filmed at a different baking landmark. When Bakewell puddings were on the menu, the competition fittingly moved to Bakewell in Derbyshire, where the eponymous tart was first made by accident in 1820, by a chef at a pub called the White Horse Inn, after he messed up a recipe given to him by the landlady. Mini documentary-style films about the history of baking were also woven into the show.

It sounds nice and genteel – but, of course, this was also a competition. Each week the contestant whose culinary skills were most lacking was ejected from the show, until the 12 were whittled down to a single winner. There were tears over the tinfoil, curses into the clingfilm and breakdowns by the baking trays. The gentle pursuit of baking got the full reality-show treatment.

It was a formula that had worked so well before, and the producers hoped it would mirror the success of other competitive cooking shows. The long-running *MasterChef*, which was on screens in the UK from 1990 for 11 series and later revived in 2005, had been syndicated across the globe in places as far-flung as Vietnam, Indonesia and Bangladesh. Other programmes such as ITV1's *Hell's Kitchen* had also been a ratings hit – celebrities had been pitted against each other in makeshift restaurants run by TV chefs Gordon Ramsay and, later, Marco Pierre White. Combining cooking and reality TV was proving to be a sure-fire ratings hit, and was a format that BBC commissioners felt they could take in an interesting direction. But this time it was to be different. Elaborate nouveau cuisine would be replaced with scones, Victoria sponges and treacle puddings. What wasn't to like?

But few could have anticipated that the show would become so universally loved, as quickly became the case. But while the contestants became mini-celebrities in their own right, the real fame – it would soon become clear – was reserved for the judges. As was often the case with reality shows, it was the judges who emerged as the actual stars.

When it came to picking them, it had been important to strike the right balance. Producers wanted two judges who really knew their stuff. The first to be chosen was a former professional baker, Paul Hollywood. As a man who knew his trade like the back of his hand, after learning from his father (who was also a baker), it was envisaged that Paul would be able to dispense honest advice and criticism without any showbiz airs and graces. He would be cast as the no-nonsense judge who wasn't afraid to speak his mind and throw the occasional witty put-down in the direction of an unfortunate contestant whose talents had gone awry. This was a familiar role, well defined by other competitive cookery shows. For example, *MasterChef* had Gregg Wallace, the shaven-headed restaurateur who was born and raised in the East End of London and began his career selling vegetables at a stand in Covent Garden. He regularly referred to himself as 'the fat, bald bloke on *MasterChef* who likes pudding', pulled no punches when it came to speaking his mind, and had proved incredibly popular. Similarly, Gordon Ramsay's TV career had flourished thanks in part to his uncompromising perfectionism and infamous short temper on *Hell's Kitchen*, his first prime-time reality show. His use of expletives during confrontations with contestants paid no heed to the fact that they were celebrities. The concept of a mercurial, mouthy chef daring to flamboyantly criticise famous soap stars, singers and actors for producing below-par food was lapped up by viewers. And so, with his straightforward and honest manner, Paul Hollywood would fit the bill for *Bake Off* perfectly, the producers decided.

However, the producers also wanted someone to complement Paul ... someone familiar to viewers; a sympathetic character who knew what they were talking about, but who could also let the contestants down gently when their baking wasn't up to scratch. There needed to be balance – a gentler, female presence on the show; a person who was equally capable in the kitchen but perhaps a touch more diplomatic. After much brainstorming, the producers kept coming back to one name – Mary Berry.

MARY BERRY: QUEEN OF BRITISH BAKING

This world-renowned and celebrated cookery writer was loved and respected by the British public in equal measure. Since the late 1960s Mary Berry's books had flown off the shelves. She had written more than 70 titles, which between then had sold in excess of 5 million copies. She had become a popular fixture on TV and radio, dispensing advice to would-be homemakers and carrying out cookery demonstrations. She had written widely for newspapers and magazines across several decades. She was the so-called Queen of the Aga, having run cookery classes custom-designed for the iconic stove from her own kitchen. On top of that, she had travelled the length and breadth of the country, cooking for live audiences, as well as lending time to support her favourite charities. Baking, she said, had helped her through some of the hardest times in her life as well as helping her celebrate some of the happiest. And as a trusted, kind woman in her seventies, she had wide appeal across the age groups, right up to the older demographic the show was hoping to capture. Mary Berry seemed like the perfect choice of presenter.

To the producers' delight, Mary agreed and signed up for the show.

It would be her job, alongside Paul, to taste the recipes and help give feedback to the contestants. The two would also have the final say on who stayed each week ... and who went. Their partnership seemed to work instantly and they appeared to complement each other perfectly. Many television critics agreed that the chemistry between Mary and Paul made the show an instant success. Reviews were overwhelmingly positive. And Mary, who had been off TV screens for some years, and busy writing more and more cookery books, was suddenly reinvented as a prime-time star. She took to the role like a duck to water and appeared to have the critics eating out of the palm of her hand.

'Mary has firmly established herself as the doyenne of cakes and no-frills Aga cooking,' Sarah Rainey wrote in the *Daily Telegraph*. 'The true star of the *Great British Bake Off*, she has captured the hearts of millions with her polite, no-nonsense judging style, critiquing contestants' "soggy bottoms" and "uneven bakes" – but always with a smile.'

Michael Hogan in the *Observer* was also adamant that Mary was the stand-out star. 'The *Great British Bake Off* proved a surprise hit last autumn, pulling in 5 million viewers,' he mused. 'Its queen bee is food writer Mary Berry. This doyenne of dough has had her face pressed to the oven door for 50 years and has published 40-plus cookbooks. She and her co-judge, the brilliantly named Paul Hollywood, get down on their haunches to peer at contestants' confections, poke them to rate "the quality of the bake", then diagnose faults with forensic honesty. Berry is unfailingly polite, deploying a withering look of disappointment, like a badly letdown home economics teacher.'

And the praise just kept coming. Sadie Nicholas in the *Daily Express* was equally gushing. She wrote: 'It's become something of a guilty pleasure, for the *Great British Bake Off* is deliciously moreish, feelgood television at its best. However, unlike other competitive and highly successful food programmes – *MasterChef* and the *Great British Menu* to name but two – *GBBO* offers something altogether more, well, British and genteel, its format evoking images of village fêtes and afternoon teas. Nostalgia plays a huge part in the success of the programme ... After all, baking was the first experience that many of us will have had in the kitchen as children.'

As if that wasn't enough, Vicky Frost in the *Guardian* added: 'Judges Mary Berry and Paul Hollywood come from the toughbutfair school of television experts. There is little emotional discussion of the contestants' journey to get this far in the competition, it is entirely about the bake ... Berry can spot an incorrectly rolled roulade at 20 paces. Both provide masses of hints and tips for getting it right.'

High praise if ever there was any. But while the critics were unanimous, so were the viewers. A search of Mary Berry's name on Google returns no fewer than 33.6 million results, with hundreds of fan pages cropping up across the Internet, including on popular social networking sites such as Facebook. 'She's such a lovely woman, like the best grand-mother in the world,' says one fan. Another adds: 'How can anyone be 77, make a living eating cake and look that good in jeans?' One blogger has even dedicated a whole site to photos of Mary biting into cakes; such is the obsession with TV's most unlikely star. Captions on the blog include: 'Now here's a rare bite for you to check off in your I-Spy book of British Bites. Here, Mary uses her little-documented telepathic power to orchestrate a beautiful synchrobite with the all-too-susceptible Paul.' It's fairly apparent that the website is to be read with a large dose of irony. But it indicates just how large Mary's cult following has become. And this fan base looks set to grow as the *Great British Bake Off* continues its run.

But while Mary's star was on the rise once again, it appeared that Janet's croissants hadn't risen quite as she had hoped. Alongside housewife and grandmother-of-three

Janet Basu, who hailed from Southport, Merseyside, were Mary-Anne Boermans, Holly Bell and Joanne Wheatley. All of them had sweated blood and tears to get to this stage and, during that process, Janet had emerged as the favourite. Viewers adored her, not least because of her down-to-earth personality. When contestants had to make pork pies with quails' eggs, Janet made no bones about the fact that she had simpler tastes. 'I'm not grand like Henry VIII, living on quails' eggs and larks' tongues,' she said. And she had been self-deprecating while comparing herself to her rivals. 'Jo was sitting there looking demure and elegant before I'd even crushed my silly biscuits,' said Janet, referring to Joanne, who would eventually go on to triumph and win the second series. In the world of fly-on-the-wall TV, Janet was a viewers' favourite – someone whom they could empathise with.

Her personality aside, Janet's skills in the kitchen were brilliant too. Her cheesecake reigned supreme, her cookies were the best by far and her torte was good enough for a Michelin-starred restaurant, she was told. But then something went wrong. As she approached the finish line, problems emerged. Her chocolate roulade, a tricky recipe for even the most seasoned of bakers to get right, disintegrated into a mound of crumbs. She was given a second chance and it all came down to her final dish – pastries. And as Mary Berry tasted them it was clear she wasn't impressed. Janet's iced buns and croissants were ranked bottom out of the four contestants. In her typically droll fashion, the show's co-presenter Mel Giedroyc said that Janet's croissants 'look like a neck support'. The writing seemed to be on the wall for Janet. Despite all the good she had done up until that point, the judges' decision was final. She was sent home, hanging up her apron and turning off her oven for the last time.

But as is often the case with reality shows, that wasn't the end. Critics were up in arms about Janet's axing. It was, they suggested, brutal and unfair – she should have been given another chance.

Sarah Rainey in the *Daily Telegraph* even admitted to shedding tears over Janet's demise. She wrote that Janet had 'become a big part of my life over the past eight weeks. Despite her best efforts to roll the sponge into a spiral, the unruly pudding fell apart, spilling whipped cream everywhere, leaving Janet – and me – reaching for a hanky.' She added, 'A crumb out of place, an over-baked pastry or a misshapen biscuit is enough for a contestant to be sent back to baking obscurity. Just look at what happened to poor Janet.'

In the tough world of reality TV, no one, not even a kindly grandmother from the northwest, is safe. Mary herself admitted she was surprised by the reaction, not least from her own relatives. Mary, a grandmother of five herself, says the youngsters in her family were beside themselves when Janet got the boot. 'They watch the programme, and I had one phone call from Gracie absolutely sobbing, "Granny, why did you send Janet home?"' Mary told *Desert Island Discs*. '"We love Janet. You're wrong!"'

Perhaps Mary, the gentle middle-class mayor's daughter, had a more cut-throat side than her public credited her with? Could she, in fact, have unwittingly and against all expectations become the latest TV cook to turn nasty on a reality show? Perhaps the producers had got her and Paul's roles mixed up? Mary laughed off the suggestion. 'Simon

Cowell, watch out!' she giggled, referring to the mogul behind the international TV singing competition *The X Factor* in an interview with the *Daily Express*. But while Mary may have achieved newfound fame thanks to her role as TV judge, she insists her principles still remain the same as when she first started out in the industry as a recipe tester for a string of London-based firms. Her judging style, she says, is as sickly-sweet as her treacle sponge recipe. 'I don't want to be unkind to the contestants, because it might put people off,' Mary told the *Daily Express*. 'The dramas happen naturally when people drop and burn things. We don't want loads of tears and whatever. I'm there to comfort them and to say, "Come on, let's mend it or do it again."'

It's fair to say that the landscape of television has changed considerably since Mary first appeared on the box on Judith Chalmers's teatime talkshow *Afternoon Plus* in the 1970s. Fierce competition, real-life dramas and fly-on-the-wall scenarios became the bread and butter of modern TV hits during the 2000s, something Mary had never been a part of ... until *GBBO* came knocking.

But it appears that the reason for Mary's popularity on the show, agreed on by viewers and critics, is that Mary refuses to conform to any stereotypes of what a reality TV judge should be. Quite simply, she is herself – the same person the British public fell in love with when she released her first cookery book more than 40 years before the show hit our screens. Episodes like Janet's dismissal aside, Mary maintains that her approach to the role of judging is very different to Paul's. They are from different walks of life – Mary came from a middle-class family before studying at Le Cordon Bleu in Paris and domestic science at her local college in

Bath, while Paul learnt from his father in the family bakery before setting up shop by himself. Mary says she's more than happy for her colleague to take on the role of the tough-talking judge, while she continues to be more nurturing. 'Paul is more exacting,' Mary told the *Daily Express*. 'I don't care if it would make better TV for me to be unkind. We want people to be encouraged to bake.'

And it appears that Mary's kindly approach has achieved just that. Supermarket chain Morrisons claims that the *Great British Bake Off* has prompted millions of sweet-toothed viewers to get busy in the kitchen. Sales of baking trays rose by 25 per cent during the second series, while sales of ingredients were up 10 per cent. More than 23,000kg of flour and 2,200kg of marzipan were shifted in the space of one week. Shoppers also bought 360 litres of vanilla extract and 15,000 bottles of food colouring. A spokesman for the chain said: 'We thought the show would inspire the nation so we made sure our baking aisle was fully stocked. It's a good job we did, given the sales increase.' Meanwhile, during the second series of *GBBO*, John Lewis reported that since the show had begun that August, sales of cake tins and muffin trays had risen by 15 per cent, and cookie cutters and cake stands by 10 per cent. This wasn't a new phenomenon, though. Supermarkets had long since become accustomed to what became known as the 'Delia Effect', where products used by much-loved celebrity cook Delia Smith on her programmes, such as limes and cranberries, had flown off the shelves. But the *Great British Bake Off* was the first time anyone could remember baking staples selling in such vast quantities, and so quickly. If ever there was a test of popularity for a TV programme, this was it.

On top of that, for the third series, a record 7,000 amateur bakers applied to join the competition – up from the 1,000 who had auditioned for the inaugural series. The show itself had been extended to twelve weeks instead of eight for the second series after producers saw how popular it was becoming. More masterclass episodes were added, too, with Paul and Mary showing the nation how certain iconic dishes should be cooked. Britain, it seemed, had gone crazy for the *Great British Bake Off*.

For her part, Mary is clearly enjoying the show's success. While she's been respected by her devotees for decades, she's since been introduced to new generations of fans, who perhaps would only have known about Mary through their parents' – or even their grandparents' – cookbooks. And Mary's success as a TV judge is set to continue. *Junior Bake Off* and *Celebrity Bake Off* to raise money for charity have also been commissioned. Spin-off documentaries from the *Great British Bake Off,* which Mary has hosted alongside Paul, have also been a hit. More books are in the pipeline and her product line is set to expand.

But Mary insists that, despite her age, she's far from done. 'An awful lot of people who watch *Bake Off* are actually cooking, which is wonderful,' she told the *Daily Express*. 'I come from a strong stock of people who enjoy what they do. My mother was 105 when she died, so you've got me for a bit yet. I enjoy what I do and so I do it. I feel lucky to be asked.'

Working is what Mary has always done best. Relentlessly, throughout her adult life, she has – perhaps almost inadvertently – grafted her way to the top of the cookery industry in Britain. She has never rested on her laurels, despite her success, and has been driven by her love of baking to keep on going. 'I just love every single working day, whether I'm writing a cookery book, doing an Aga cookery demonstration or presenting cookery on TV,' she said in 2007 in an interview with the *Scotsman*. 'As soon as I left school I knew I wanted to pursue my passion for food and cooking. I was determined to take advantage of every opportunity that came my way. In college holidays I worked, hands on, for spells in a butcher's, a baker's and a fish shop. Along the way I did, and still do, try my very best, but I make sure that I enjoy it too.' So while it may seem that *GBBO* has made Mary a star, the reality is that she was a force to be reckoned with long before the show was commissioned.

After spending years working as a cook, Mary appeared to be in the right place at the right time as baking swung back into fashion the length and breadth of Britain. As the recession loomed and the doom and gloom of the economic crisis dominated newspaper front pages, people started looking for cheap, quick ways to cook up treats in the kitchen. Baking was the obvious choice. Rather than forking out hard-earned money on mass-produced cakes, biscuits and pastries, it seemed the obvious way to cost-cut while also continuing to enjoy the sweeter things in life. Handmade was suddenly back in vogue. Mary told the *Daily Mail* how important decent food is during hard times, and that it isn't necessarily a difficult thing to eat well when times are tough: 'People are a bit hard up now, with the financial crisis. Fortunately, home-made presents are appreciated so much more than flowers or chocolates. Everyone is chuffed to bits to get a jar of marmalade or a batch of buns. The other week, I was giving a talk to the Women's Institute in Darlington and an elderly lady in the audience came up and gave me a box of biscuits she'd made. I could have wept.' Other commentators suggested that the return to baking coincided with a return to the older values of bygone eras. While during the 1990s, many women embraced the concept of 'girl power' and rejected the usual stereotypes of staying at home, looking after the children and knowing their way around the kitchen, suddenly women appeared happy to play homemaker again.

This return to retro values from the 1950s and 1960s gave baking a new lease of life that few could have predicted. Anne Harrison, chairman of Denman College, where the Women's Institute cookery school is run, and vice chairman of the Women's Institute board of trustees, told the *Daily Telegraph*: 'Twenty years ago, baking was not popular – it was almost frowned upon. Now the craft of baking has come back into fashion. My granddaughter bakes, and recipes are being passed down through the generations.' Mary has her own theories as to why baking has had such a huge resurgence in popularity in recent years. 'Well, it used to be a bit plain, but since the fashion for cupcakes it's become glamorous,' Mary told *Stella* magazine. 'But it's also about the recession. How much does it cost to take your children to Legoland? You could spend the afternoon baking, which is very cheap, and you've taught them something, and you have a lovely quiche or some scones to eat afterwards.' She added in an interview with the *Daily Mail*: 'It's a bit of joy in the middle of this recession. You watch a programme like this and begin to feel warm again. It's what life is all about. Even if money is short, it doesn't cost much to bake a scone. If you're feeling a little bit down, a little bit of kneading really helps.'

Whatever the reason for baking's return to fashion, Mary couldn't be more delighted that it appears to have been embraced by the British public once again. 'There is tremendous interest in home baking,' she told the *Daily Telegraph*. 'And more people are realising that it is something that is enjoyed by all the family. Cook with the young on a rainy day, and it is educational: with all this weighing and measuring, it really teaches them something.' But for Mary, baking is more than just producing cakes and pastries. It's a way of life, and one that has been ingrained in her over decades. Baking transformed Mary from a wannabe cook into a household name, thanks to her cookbooks, product lines and TV appearances. But it has also taught her some of life's most important lessons. She has long been an advocate of baking as 'therapy' and she freely admits it has helped calm her and understand the ways of the world during difficult moments. It's also allowed her to connect with other people, she says. Most of all, it simply puts a smile on her face.

She summed up the power of baking poignantly in a piece she published in the *Daily Mail*. Mary wrote: 'Baking ... keeps us connected with other people, which is terribly important as we get older. I'm always struck by how many contestants on the *Great British Bake Off* say they were first inspired to bake by their grandmother. There is often a deep connection there, and a treasured link to previous generations as family recipes are passed down. Older people often feel they're not as needed or as useful as they once were, so to be able to contribute – by saying, for example, "I made this shortbread" when you serve it to visitors – is a huge reward. I have often been asked if other people bake for me, probably because they imagine anyone might run a mile from presenting Mary Berry with a Victoria sponge cake, in case I judge it. But I love to eat anything home-made. A friend gave me some jam the other day, and it was wonderful. She also brought along a few slices of her Christmas cake, which was still delicious, and I was delighted. For me, a home-baked gift is miles better than a bunch of flowers or a box of chocolates, because it involves thought, planning and time. And how can it be anything but good for us to indulge in something that brings such pleasure to the giver and to the receiver?'

It is, therefore, easy to understand why Mary is so nurturing as a TV judge: in her view baking shouldn't be divisive, but rather a uniting force. And whether or not she's on television, baking will always be part of her life. While Mary Berry may be the latest cook to achieve TV stardom, it's safe to say that baking has also made her the nicest. She has refused to let being a judge change her day-to-day life ... and that includes her relationships with her closest friends, with whom she enjoys sharing the rich delights of baking.

And with a philosophy like that, it's no wonder that Mary is Britain's best-loved baker. She is unrivalled in her knowledge of cakes, and loved by thousands for her kind, gentle personality. Mary is, quite simply, the undisputed Queen of British Baking.

CHAPTER 2

EARLY LIFE

Mary Berry vividly remembers her childhood – and it's easy to understand why. Despite partly growing up during the doom and gloom of the Second World War, it was seemingly an idyllic existence. 'I remember during the war; I remember the house, the garden,' she said to Kirsty Young when she appeared on *Desert Island Discs* in 2012. 'It's funny, even when I was very small, I can remember the three gardens that we had; I can remember almost every plant in them.' Her parents Margaret and Alleyne worked tirelessly to make sure Mary and her two brothers never went without. Growing up on a large estate in Bath, Mary's childhood consisted of great-outdoors adventures in the surrounding sprawling countryside, and opportunities that very few children her age were privileged enough to have.

It's fair to say that Mary's parents wanted to give her the good upbringing they had both enjoyed. Both of Mary's parents came from very comfortable backgrounds. Born in 1905 in Stanley Bridge, Lancashire, Mary's mother Margaret was one of four children. She attended Harrogate College in North Yorkshire. Her parents ordered her to study elocution, so desperate were they for her to lose her northern accent and forge a career for herself away from the county, where they believed there were no prospects for her. They got their wish – after completing her studies, Margaret moved to Manchester and managed to get regular work as a jobbing actress in opera and theatre. Her charisma and love of fine clothes earned her a glamorous reputation and quickly made her a well-known name on the circuit. Eventually she got to the point where she took the lead role once a year at the Manchester Opera House.

By the mid-1920s Margaret had met Alleyne Berry at a dance in St Albans, Hertfordshire. As was typical in those days, a relatively short courtship followed before Alleyne proposed. They married in 1929 in a lavish ceremony in Manchester Cathedral before moving to the pretty town of Otley, North Yorkshire, where the couple set up home. They only stayed there a short while before moving south to the Roman spa town of Bath in 1932, soon after the birth of their first son, Roger. The Berrys believed life would be more exciting in the West Country, and also felt there would be more opportunities for both themselves and their family than in sleepy Yorkshire.

Bath, with its rich cultural history and exciting metropolitan atmosphere, seemed like the perfect place for them. A city on the banks of the River Avon in southwest England with a current population of around 84,000, Bath was established by the Romans as Aquae Sulis in around AD

43. The invading army was attracted by its natural hot springs – the only hot springs in Britain – which they believed had healing properties. The Romans built a lavish bath complex to take advantage of this precious water, which rose up naturally through the surrounding limestone, and their example was followed in Georgian times when Bath became a popular spa destination. The heritage of beautiful Georgian architecture built from the local Bath stone is evident throughout the city to this day. It attracts more than 4 million tourists every year, who take in the Roman Baths, as well as visiting the Fashion Museum and immersing themselves in the world of Jane Austen, one of the city's other famous residents. In 1987 the city became a UNESCO World Heritage Site.

It is easy to see what appealed to Margaret and Alleyne about the city, with its picturesque architecture and abundance of green space. They must have envisaged family outings around the town, perhaps relaxing on a Sunday afternoon with the crowds in Royal Victoria Park, opened in 1830 by the 11-year-old Princess Victoria, which covers 57 acres and includes botanical gardens, golf courses and a replica Roman temple that was displayed at the British Empire Exhibition at Wembley in 1924. Or perhaps swimming in Beau Street's public swimming pool, built in 1923. Between 1904 and 1939, the city even had a network of electric trams running through its streets, adding to the pleasant atmosphere.

Bath was also a city with a sense of civic duty – thousands of wounded soldiers were rehabilitated in spa towns such as Bath following the First World War. During the Second World War, the Ministry of Defence's naval department took over key buildings in the town from which to coordinate the war effort.

When Mary was growing up, the city was recovering from the shock of being targeted by the Luftwaffe during a campaign known as the Baedeker Blitz. Between 25 and 27 April 1942, German bombers carried out three air raids in reprisal for RAF raids on the German cities of Lübeck and Rostock, damaging more than 19,000 buildings in the city and killing 21 residents. But civic pride and spirit meant that the damage was soon repaired.

Once they had relocated to Bath, Mary's parents were keen to give both themselves and their future family the best possible start in life. Alleyne, a trained surveyor, set up the business that was later to become Berry, Powell and Shackell; he ran it out of the back of an old post office in Bath. Despite its humble beginnings, his auctioneering and valuation firm grew to become one of the largest such firms in the southwest of England. As was typical in the 1930s, Margaret, a keen bridge player, was a housewife, but would often help her husband part-time with the business's bookkeeping and accounts. But while the business eventually became a big success, in years when they were building it up times weren't always easy. Mary recalls how her father, a keen photographer, won a £100 prize from a local newspaper after he sent in a snap he had taken of Margaret on a seesaw on the beach for Mary and her brother Roger. In 1938, when Alleyne won the competition, £100 was a princely sum, and Mary's father would often tell her 'You don't know what it meant to us,' for years after. Mary's family understood the value of money and tried their best to instil this ethos in her from a young age.

Aside from their careers and family responsibilities, Alleyne and Margaret threw themselves into Bath's public life, too. Both were determined to make as big an impact as possible. Very quickly, they climbed the social ranks and became pillars of the city's affluent, middle-class community. Alleyne became a councillor before the Second World War, serving on all the council's main committees, including Town and Country Planning. He was also the founding chairman of the Bath Round Table, and the founding member of the Bass Assembly, which would later become the Bath International Music Festival. To this day the festival continues and has become an annual event. Lasting 12 days, usually from late May to early June, it brings together an eclectic variety of music. This includes orchestral and classical virtuosi, and jazz, folk and world musicians playing individually and in groups. Alleyne's dedication to civic duties paid off. He later went on to become Mayor of Bath between 1953 and 1954 and, as a result, Margaret was made Lady Mayoress. The couple were at the heart of Bath's civic community and were invited to every important dinner party, event or function going. However, their relationship would always come first.

When Alleyne was invited to America while he was Mayor, he insisted that he couldn't go unless his wife came too. Her son (Mary's brother, William) told the *Bath Chronicle*: 'Father was asked to go to America, but said he never went anywhere without his wife – so they told him to bring her too. When they were in America they were given the president's bodyguard to look after them.'

After finishing his tenure as Mayor, Alleyne was closely involved in establishing the University of Bath at Claverton

Down. The institution went on to become one of the world's most respected for teaching sciences and modern languages to degree level. Years later, in 1979, Alleyne was awarded an honorary degree (an MA) to thank him for his tireless work for the university and the city.

This stern and serious public persona was evident in his home life, according to Mary. 'My father was a very strong person,' says Mary. 'He was not affectionate towards us. He was very strict. But he did things with us. He was a great man; he was very involved with Bath. And he encouraged Bath to have a university. He was a surveyor and he was chairman of planning. So he found the land for Bath University on Claverton Down and persuaded the powers that be that there should be a university.'

By no means did Margaret take a back seat when it came to public duties. She was the founding chairman of the Friends of the Royal United Hospital in Bath, a charity which supported the work of doctors and nurses. Later she was appointed chairwoman of the Townswomen's Guild and the Inner Wheel. Her local standing and popularity were such that her 100th birthday in 2005 was covered prominently by the *Bath Chronicle*. The celebrations were held at the city's Guildhall by the then Mayor of Bath, Peter Metcalfe, who hosted an afternoon tea in the Mayor's Parlour, along with past and present dignitaries from Bath and North East Somerset Council. Margaret and her family then moved on to the plush Priory Hotel for a family celebration. At the celebrations, Margaret said: 'I've had a great deal to be thankful for.'

The gratitude Margaret expressed at her birthday doubtless included a reference to her family. Aside from all the work to build up the business and to fulfil their public duties, Margaret and Alleyne soon set about expanding their family. After Roger came William, before Mary was born on 24 March 1935.

Mary recalls growing up on a sprawling estate in the Avon countryside, where life was always an adventure. She recalls her earliest memory as being a fishing trip with her father. She told the *Scotsman*: 'I think it'd be catching a mackerel with my dad when I was around four years old.' Other memories were perhaps not so idyllic, but nevertheless show how the family threw themselves into rural life. She said in another interview: 'When I was five or six years old, we had baby chicks. A lamp caught fire and they all died. It was a horrible shock, which I suppose is why I remember it.'

And as Alleyne's business interests went from strength to strength, he was able to splash out occasionally on luxuries other families couldn't afford. One was a boat – something very few middle-class families had in the 1930s.

'Dad always had a hobby of something,' Mary said in her interview on *Desert Island Discs*. 'He built a boat that we kept near Bath when we'd moved and it was on the river and we used to go every weekend. We didn't sail; we had oars. And you know, that was great entertainment. We'd arrive and there would be a Primus, which usually didn't work too well, and you'd make tea and you'd have sandwiches. It was a great way of being amused. But in those days, you know, the seasons you had "primrosing", we used to go and pick primroses and take a picnic. Then we would go and pick blackberries and again there were picnics.'

Mary and her brothers would often while away the days in

the acres of land surrounding their home, building secret dens where they spent hours on end.

'And can you imagine health and safety nowadays?' said Mary. 'We lit a fire, made with bricks at the side, and then there was a pipe, a curved pipe that went through and we poured water from the top and it came out into a bucket. I mean, I don't even know if our parents knew about it! You could get into corners of the garden where you wouldn't be found. Or the goat pen would be a great place to go and hide.'

And although she didn't discover her love of cooking until much later in her teenage years, Mary admits that family meals during her childhood helped form the basis of what would become her future career. Her mother Margaret was a keen cook ... and Mary freely admits that she herself had a voracious appetite. Mary and her brothers were often encouraged to get involved with the preparation of meals, which were very much family affairs. 'I was a chubby child and loved my food,' she said in an interview. 'And no wonder – Mum made such good things: boiled salt beef and carrots, steak and kidney, and a delicious bread-and-butter pudding. We didn't have many toys, but loved helping round the house, chopping vegetables and laying the table.' Mary added, in an interview with the *Daily Mail*: 'My mother wasn't a cook by trade, but we always had home-cooked everything.' It also appears possible to trace Mary's love of desserts, puddings and cakes back to her mother's habits in the kitchen. Mary recalls the precise recipes that her mother used. 'Her bread-and-butter pudding brings back such memories; her secret was to add the grated rind of a lemon and half a teaspoon of mixed spice and to let the pudding stand, sprinkled with demerara sugar, for an hour before baking.' Mary admits that there are other foods that, if she tastes even today, bring back vivid memories of her mother's cooking. 'When I have the first fresh taste of the season's marmalade that I have made, it takes me back to the days of my mother making marmalade,' she said in an interview with the *Financial Times*. 'I minced the peel for her – she was always very busy. She had a big kitchen in our house in Bath, with a huge scrubbed wooden table, a gas stove and a temperamental hot water supply. There were few gadgets – mincers, sharp knives – so it was simple, but a lot went on in it.'

The deep sense of routine surrounding mealtimes was something that would live with Mary for the rest of her life. Even today she regularly speaks about how she believes it is important for families to value mealtimes in order to bring them closer together. 'All our meals were round the table, and I think that's perhaps what's missing now,' she has said. 'Even now when we all sit round, the tummies are full, and then the children begin to tell you a bit about their life when they're happy, and I think it's very sad that so many people have meals every day by the television. It is not at all easy. But it is nice to plan an occasion, once a week, when you are all together. I think it's a great way of communicating.'

Yet Mary was also a child of the Second World War. Children growing up during that time had a very different childhood from those today. Lessons at school were supplemented by classes about how to put on gas masks, and punctuated by air-raid drills. People were encouraged to be thrifty and to save everything – even bath water was restricted to five inches per family per week. Many children living in rural areas found themselves with new playmates, as evacuees from the cities were billeted in any home with room to spare, and gardens were dug up to provide air-raid shelters for their owners.

Perhaps the most noticeable change in lifestyle for the Berrys would have been food rationing. This was a key part of Mary's childhood, with Margaret and Alleyne issued with booklets for everyone in the family – beige for the adults, and pink for each child.

As the Second World War began, Britain was importing 70 per cent of its food. That meant that boats bringing supplies to the island were a prime target for Axis attacks. So Britain needed both to become more self-sufficient, and to make sure that, as supplies dropped, price rises didn't leave the poorest members of society unable to eat.

Food rationing was introduced in the UK in January 1940, with restrictions covering more and more items as the war progressed. Wasting food became a criminal offence. Each person had to register at their chosen shops and take their ration book with them, which contained coupons for certain amounts of food. A typical ration for one adult per week was 2oz butter, 4oz bacon and ham, 4oz margarine, 8oz sugar, meat to the value of 1s.2d (about 6p today), 2–3 pints of milk, 2oz cheese, 1 egg and 2oz tea. They could also have 1lb of jam every two months, a packet of dried eggs every four weeks, and 12oz sweets every four weeks.

Although the menu seems restricted to modern appetites, some nutritionists say the diet actually improved the nation's health. On average, children became taller and heavier than before the war, and incidences of anaemia and tooth decay both dropped.

Some things were simply unobtainable – lemons and bananas all but disappeared from Britain's shops, and oranges were generally reserved for children and pregnant women. These limitations meant that everything had to be made from scratch – an approach still dear to Mary today. And people became ingenious at creating substitute items for products they missed. Children might be given a raw carrot on a stick in place of ice cream, and 'cream' was mocked up by mixing margarine, milk and cornflour. If Mary had been older, perhaps she would have been on the wireless dishing out cooking tips like Marguerite Patten, whose show on the Home Service attracted 6 million listeners a day.

It was not just food that was rationed. Clothing was issued on a points system, with the allowance initially covering approximately one new outfit a year. By the end of the war, buying a coat would cost almost a year's coupons. Women would paint gravy browning on their legs in place of silk stockings. Petrol was also rationed, and from 1942 it was restricted to 'official' users such as the emergency services, farmers and bus companies. Like all families, this affected the Berrys, which made getting around – to and from work, on shopping trips with their books of coupons, to visit friends – a tricky process.

Rationing even continued beyond the end of the war, partly to help feed people in European areas under British control. In some cases it became stricter – bread had not been formally rationed, but it was between 1946 and 1948, while potato rationing began in 1947. Rationing was gradually withdrawn from 1950 onwards, finally ending on 4 July

1954, when meat became freely available again. Alongside rationing, the Ministry of Food launched a pioneering campaign called Dig For Victory. This was meant to promote self-sufficiency, with people being encouraged to grow their own fruit and vegetables and even keep domesticated pigs, chickens and rabbits for their meat. With their large garden, the Berrys were keen adherents to a self-sufficient lifestyle, keeping goats and a pig. 'The pig would be fattened and then it would go to be slaughtered, and come back to us. I think we shared it with a neighbour,' Mary remembered on *Desert Island Discs*.

Irrespective of the trials and tribulations of the war, it's fair to say that family life was nothing short of blissful, though Mary also had a rebellious streak. On one occasion she uprooted dozens of carefully tended flowers from the family garden before trying to sell them for profit. Unsurprisingly, Alleyne was not impressed when he returned home from one of his civic duties.

'I remember, we had lovely flowers in the garden and I was at home in the school holidays and I picked flowers from the garden, did them in bunches, and set up a stall outside with no permission whatsoever,' she recalled. 'Then Dad came back on his motorbike, because you weren't allowed cars in the war and we had no petrol, and I was scolded and Dad said, well, this afternoon you go across to Miss Jackson, who raised money for the Red Cross, and you give all that money to the Red Cross.'

Hardly the crime of the century, but her aptitude for being 'naughty' as she described it in later interviews seemed to be getting in full swing by the time she was ready to start attending secondary school at the age of 11. Mary's parents enrolled her in Bath High, the local all-girls public school. Other high-profile pupils who have attended the school include suffragette Mary Blathwayt, stage actress and singer Joan Heal, Elizabeth Hallam Smith, who was made the Librarian of the House of Lords in 2006, Marguerite Bowie, who organised the evacuation of children to the USA and Canada in 1939, and Elspeth Howe, Baroness Howe of Idlicote CBE, wife of Geoffrey Howe and Chairman from 1997 to 1999 of the Broadcasting Standards Commission.

It is an impressive pedigree by anyone's standards. But while Mary's name now sits at the very top of the school's list of famous alumni, her teachers at the time would never have predicted that would be the case. It's safe to say that Mary was not a model student – in fact, quite the opposite. Despite her parents' best efforts to send her to a good school, Mary freely admits she just wasn't interested in her studies. Her work ethic was somewhat lacking, to say the least; so much so that her teachers went as far as to describe her academic abilities as 'hopeless'. She shirked homework, was rarely on time in the morning and was consistently bottom – or very near bottom – of the class. Mary freely admits she often got preoccupied. 'I was a real monkey, hopeless at academic subjects. I was quite naughty – don't tell my children!' She says she's never been a regular smoker, but that she did try it once, with her brothers in the goat shed.

Considering he was a man of great achievement and social standing, Alleyne was somewhat disappointed by Mary's lacklustre performance at school. He had always been an academic high-flyer and expected the same of his children. Looking back, Mary admits she should have been more focused.

'To be honest, I think he was immensely disappointed that I wasn't academic,' says Mary. 'He was just, really just sad about it. Didn't do anything about it, and I didn't work at school, which I think is really sad that I didn't, and I regret it. But I have worked very, very hard since.'

However, Mary's aptitude for making things was clear at that young age ... even if it wasn't cakes at that point. While she may not have been the most academic girl, she had a flair for creativity at home. 'I do remember when I was about 12 I made a rag doll, and I made it beautifully,' she says. 'And dad said, where did you get that from, and I said, "I made it." And he gave me a shilling, 5p, and I can't ever remember being rewarded for doing something and I was really chuffed about that.'

While it soon became apparent she was no good at the more traditional academic subjects, one teacher, Miss Date, noticed her flair for cooking. Her mother had always loved baking and cooking at home, but Mary rarely got involved beyond the most basic food preparation tasks to help out Margaret. She only discovered it while she was picking subjects at school to take to examination level. Little did rebellious, work-shy Mary realise that this was to become the start of a long and highly successful career. 'My first cooking really was at school. It came to the choice of subjects for school cert,' Mary explained on *Desert Island Discs*. 'And those clever people did Latin and Maths, and the dim people did Domestic Science. But from the moment I did Domestic Science I absolutely loved it.'

Mary experienced what she describes as a 'eureka moment'. Speaking to the *Daily Telegraph*, she added: 'It was all "could try harder" until I gave up Latin and Maths and went to the Domestic Science department. Miss Date was the teacher and she was wonderful! Miss Date praised me, she helped me, she encouraged me.'

Mary's success in the subject was almost immediate. She appeared to be a natural, standing head and shoulders above the other students. She vividly remembers the first thing she cooked in the school kitchen. It was treacle sponge pudding – and it went down a treat with Miss Date. Not only was this the first bit of praise she had received from a schoolteacher, but, most telling of all, it got the seal of approval from her usually stern and standoffish father, who suddenly realised that his daughter wasn't a lost cause. The feeling of acceptance Mary finally felt from her father about something relating to her schoolwork has stayed with her to this day.

'I can remember bringing home the first thing I made there – a treacle sponge pudding,' says Mary. 'I reheated it, turned it out and the golden syrup poured down the sides. Dad tasted it and said, "That's really good, as good as Mummy's." Well, what did I feel like? Wonderful!'

However, it was ironic that her love for cooking started at school, Mary would later say ... because the school dinners were nothing to write home about. 'You didn't notice too much what it was,' she told the *Financial Times*. 'You stopped at one o'clock for lunch and you just accepted it and ate it. I can always remember the sliced meat and gravy, and one enjoyed the classic, proper puddings. The home economics lessons at Bath High School were absolutely brilliant, however. That's the whole reason I am where I am today.'

But while Mary appeared to be on the up at school, her idyllic childhood was about to be brought to an abrupt halt, albeit temporarily. Soon after she celebrated her 13th birthday she contracted polio. At the time vaccination against the disease was non-existent. It wasn't until the American medical researcher Dr Jonas Salk developed a vaccination some five years later in 1952 that children were routinely injected to prevent the disease. And as a result, 13-year-old Mary faced the prospect of being paralysed for life by the viral infection. The disease can also cause meningitis and inflammation of the brain. It was a desperate situation. But as she lay limp and lifeless in bed, Mary's parents at first thought it was another attempt for her to duck out of her school work. It was only when she had been unable to leave her bed for days on end because she had lost the use of her muscles that they realised something was very seriously wrong. They rushed Mary to hospital, where the doctors quickly diagnosed her condition as polio. Even today, there is no cure for polio. But because treatment for the disease was so limited during the 1940s, they had very few options but to keep her in hospital. The whole process very quickly turned into a harrowing experience for Mary – not least because she wasn't told what was going on. 'I was sent to the isolation hospital in Bath,' says Mary. 'I was put in a room with glass sides, and so my mother could not touch me. And that is very hard. I could see her face there and I had no idea what I had got wrong with me. I didn't know. And nobody told me. That was what was so odd.' Mary even had to be fed through a cup with a spout because she was so weak that she couldn't sit up in bed.

She was kept in isolation for a month – a long time by anyone's standards, particularly for such a young girl. At that point she was then moved to a nearby orthopaedic hospital for a further two months.

To help cheer her up, and perhaps out of guilt for not taking her illness seriously in the first place, Mary's father made a grand gesture. At great expense he decided to buy her a pony ... and then brought it to the hospital for her to pet.

At the time, TB was also widespread. To treat the disease, patients were meant to get fresh air, so many hospital wards were designed so they were able to have their windows fully opened on one side. As she was recovering in the hospital's solarium, Mary noticed her dad approaching the window before he surprised her in the most extraordinary way.

'I remember my father brought my pony – can you imagine it now? Brought my pony to the hospital, walked it there, about three miles he walked with my pony so I could see it. When I was transferred to an orthopaedic hospital, Dad brought my beloved pony to the solarium so I could stroke him.'

Less than one per cent of polio patients are left with paralysis. However, while Mary made a full recovery, the left side of her body was a lot weaker than it had been before she had the condition.

'When I came home I just had this weak left side and I had my arm in a brace that held it above the head,' she recalls. 'But I recovered remarkably [though] my left hand is a bit sort of smaller and misshapen.' It affects her to this day, so that if you watch closely when Mary appears on the *Great British Bake Off*, you'll notice that her use of her left hand is limited and she often keeps it out of the direct view of the camera.

'When I'm doing television people think that I've got arthritis and they send me all sorts of cures,' she says. 'But it's not a real disadvantage; I manage well.'

She even admits that there are some advantages.

'My left hand is still a bit crumpled, but it doesn't make any difference. It just means I don't have to darn socks,' she said in one interview.

Gradually Mary fought her way back to health and in recent years has lent her support to End Polio Now, the Rotary-inspired charity that aims to eradicate the disease from the Earth. In 2011, she gave a talk to the Rotary Club of Glastonbury and Street, where all the proceeds went to the charity, speaking about how she believed it was such a good cause after everything she had been through with the disease.

After Mary recovered from polio she returned to school to complete her exams. Despite her new-found passion for Domestic Science, overall her grades were not good. And her school headmistress, Miss Blackburn, was less than complimentary during a meeting to discuss her future, and dismissed any future career prospects.

'When I left school mum and dad had to go to Miss Blackburn [and ask], you know, what career is she going to have?' says Mary. 'And Miss Blackburn said, "There is very little she could do; she could possibly look after children." And I remember dad saying, "Well, I pity the children!"'

In fact, years later in an interview with *The Lady*, Mary would say that Miss Blackburn's comments were the 'nastiest thing' anyone had ever said to her. 'When I was at school my headmistress said, "There really isn't any career that I can recommend for you. You haven't passed enough exams to do anything." That was a terrible thing to hear,' she said. Looking back on her life, Mary admits that she would have approached her studies with a bit more focus if she had her time again. Asked in an interview with the World of Books website what advice she would give to her 16-year-old self, she replied: 'Choose a vocation that you enjoy and put your all into it. Get all the experience you can and work hard – you will feel good about yourself and the rewards will come.' During the course of the meeting, though, Miss Blackburn suggested one other alternative to childcare – and that was cooking. With less-than-average grades in all her other exams, Mary realised that it was the one thing she excelled at. Not only that, it was developing into her passion; something she enjoyed outside the classroom, too. Mary agreed that cooking was the best option for her future. But she admitted that there was one other 'glamorous' job she had always wistfully dreamed of. 'I wasn't good enough for anything else really, and I didn't have an interest in anything else,' she said in an interview with the *Financial Times*. 'In those days you used to have a dream of being an air hostess – that was the glamorous job – but university wasn't really thought of unless you were terribly brainy.'

By this point her parents were pleased when Mary came up with a plan to take a catering course at Bath College of Home Economics. Although Alleyne would have preferred her to have got a professional qualification, he realised it was better for his daughter to focus on something she enjoyed. It was a formative experience, and one that Mary treasures all these years later, particularly when remembering the members of staff who opened up the world of cookery for this budding Home Ec. student, not least a Mrs Viley, who, Mary says, 'taught me lots of the basics'. It's important to continue learning and absorbing information from your peers and experts, Mary believes: 'But I've learnt from lots of chefs and cooks I've worked with. Michelle Roux Jr and Raymond Blanc, in particular, have both been influential in passing me new ideas. You never stop learning, really.' And she told the *Scotsman* about another of her inspirations: 'I'd love to have met the late Elizabeth David, just because she's the greatest ever food writer.'

She graduated with good grades after a year and whiled away the following summer in her bedroom perusing cookbooks and recipes by her favourite authors, who included Katie Stewart and Margaret and Jane Grigson, all regulars in the national press.

French influences were becoming fashionable in the late 1940s. Mary's imagination was filled with the possibilities suggested by *croque-monsieurs*, garlicky-buttery snails and truffle sauces. This ignited a desire in Mary to travel across the Channel and find out first-hand what all the fuss was about. After researching the options, Mary came across a three-month culinary course in the south of France. She was sold. But there was one problem – and that was her parents. At the time, Mary wasn't even allowed to travel to London by herself, so the prospect of travelling across the English Channel and through France was something neither of her parents were particularly keen to entertain. But, after much persuasion from Mary, they relented and her father paid for her to enrol in the Domestic Science College in Pau in the Basse-Pyrénées. Like Bath High, it was an all-girls school, but one where none of Mary's fellow students spoke any English.

However, there were other, less obvious differences to contend with.

'My French was very poor and I had to stay in a family

with ten children, and the first thing, when I got there, for our supper ... we had horse meat,' recalls Mary. 'And I had left my pony, and I can remember sobbing all the way through having to eat horse meat. Because all I could think of was what I had left at home, my pony, through the time I was at school. I was pretty homesick. I had never been away from home at all and I was very pleased to get back again.'

Despite the initial culture shock, aged 17, Mary still wanted to give France another shot and enrolled at the prestigious Le Cordon Bleu cookery school in Paris. But even attending the famous academy, where the likes of Rachel Khoo, Simone Beck, Giada De Laurentiis, Aida Mollenkamp and even the American pop star Kelis, have since learnt to become master chefs, couldn't impress Mary.

'It looked good on my CV, but it wasn't up to much in those days,' she told the *Daily Telegraph*. 'It was full of posh Americans picking up a few dishes to pass on to their cooks.' After struggling with her studies at school for almost all of her teenage years, suddenly Mary was finding it all a bit of a doddle. The exams at Le Cordon Bleu, Mary told the *Daily Mail*, were also 'dead easy', and she passed with flying colours.

She returned to Britain aged 20. And while she may not have learnt a huge amount from her time in France, she finally felt in command of the expert knowledge necessary to start climbing the ladder in the world of catering. She was desperate to move to London, but her parents banned her from doing so until she had turned 21. Even though she had lived in France for the best part of three years by herself, it was still considered a big deal to leave the family home for the capital. She admits that her relationship with her parents was somewhat different from what she later had with her own three children. 'I wasn't allowed to go to London until I was 21,' Mary recalls. 'We don't have control over our children nowadays like this! You know, Mum and Dad said you [didn't] go and that was that.'

So instead she started hunting for work back home in Bath. Eventually, after a number of job applications, she was taken on by the Electricity Board. In those days if you bought an electric cooker you could ask for a home visit from someone who would show you how it worked. And that's where Mary came in. 'I was a home-service adviser – if you bought an oven, I'd bake with you to check it was working properly,' she said in an interview with the *Daily Mail*.

The ovens Mary was demonstrating were new and exciting technology for their time. Ovens themselves were nothing new, of course. But electricity made the whole process cleaner, and it was easier to regulate temperature than it had been with the older models.

Ancient people had cooked on open fires, adding simple masonry structures to hold the food over them. Simple ovens began to appear in places such as ancient Greece to allow for cooking bread and other baked goods, and by the Middle Ages brick and mortar hearths were being built, with food usually cooked in metal cauldrons hung over the fire.

By the 1700s, inventors had begun making improvements to the stoves, mainly to contain the smoke produced by the burning wood. The fire was contained in a chamber, with holes on top for flat-bottomed cooking pans to be placed in. Around 1728, cast-iron ovens began to be made in real quantity – although they would still not have been found in the average home. Over the next century the designs evolved, offering models where the heating level of each pot could be regulated individually, as well as chimneys and flue pipes.

Coal- and kerosene-powered ovens were also introduced, but gas ovens were what really took off commercially. A British inventor called James Sharp patented a gas oven in 1826. It was the first semi-successful gas oven to hit the market, and by the 1920s most households had a gas oven with both top burners and interior ovens. In 1922, the Aga cooker, which would later play a huge part in Mary's life, was invented by Swedish Nobel Laureate Gustaf Dalén. Early electric ovens had been available from the 1890s, and one was even held up as a beacon of technological progress at the Chicago World's Fair in 1893. The first electric oven for use in homes was made in 1891 by the Carpenter Electric Heating Manufacturing Company in Minnesota, in the US Midwest.

However, the spread of electric oven technology was hindered by problems with the distribution of electricity. Elecricity had been used for communications from the late 1830s onwards, but that use only depended on the low power output of electric batteries. Scientists were struggling to scale up their laboratory discoveries to the extent required for more widespread use, and the initial investment needed to set up an electricity network was daunting, particularly when steam, gas and coal already provided satisfactory ways to produce power, light and heat.

But when Joseph Swan and Thomas Edison simultaneously invented the light bulb, it was suddenly easier to see a practical use for mains electricity. The UK's first such project came in 1881, when the streets of Godalming in Surrey were lit electrically using water power in a public test of the new technology. More and more schemes were rolled out around the country, usually set up by private companies or local authorities that had been granted statutory authority to put cables and pylons on other people's land or lay cables in the street by Acts of Parliament. By 1925, it was clear that a more efficient, national system would be a boon, and the Electricity (Supply) Act 1919 created the National Grid transmission system, linking the biggest and most efficient power stations to transfer energy around the country.

In 1936, 80 per cent of the available supply was used in industry, with 12,000 domestic homes connected to the network. Many people in rural areas objected to the building of pylons to distribute the electricity. But gradually, people were attracted by the idea of a modern, clean energy supply. By 1944, two out of three homes had electricity – the number had doubled in ten years. Having an electric oven in your home became a realistic aspiration.

While today's electric ovens come with many features including self-cleaning modes, automatic interior lighting and digital controls, the ovens Mary would have been demonstrating were much simpler affairs. But as the fifties got going, the design-conscious middle classes clamoured for ovens in bright colours with curved edges, and Britain's kitchens started to look ever more stylish.

And so Mary drove around Bath – the 'catchment area' to which she was limited to working by her parents – in the little Ford Popular the firm provided. She took with her the ingredients of a Victoria sponge, the recipe for which she already knew off by heart. To test whether an oven was working properly she would use it to whip up one of these cakes. If the cake rose properly and tasted good, she would know that the oven was in perfect working order. It was a routine that lived with Mary for years, and she later admitted that on TV shows she would often cook up the exact same cake to check that the studio's oven was functioning correctly before filming began.

Mary was finally working, and it involved cooking, but she still yearned for the bright lights of the Big Smoke. Bath, she believed, was too limiting and didn't offer her enough opportunities. 'It was fun, but I wanted to work up in London and share a flat with other girls,' said Mary.

However, that opportunity would present itself to Mary sooner than she thought. This was to be the start of a brilliant career that no one – not even her parents – could have anticipated.

CHAPTER 3

COOKING ON GAS

By the age of 22 Mary appeared to be on the brink of a big career break. Despite having struggled to find her feet with her studies, once she began to focus on her talents by working with food and people, her professional life started going swimmingly. And while she was based in Bath, she was keeping a beady eye out for any opportunities that presented themselves in London. It wasn't long before she spotted something that took her fancy – she saw an advert for a job as a cookery demonstrator for the Dutch Dairy Bureau. Mary wasted no time in applying. What more could she want? This was a job that would offer her the chance to cook for a living. Within days she was summoned for a meeting with a gentleman who was taken by Mary's passion for cooking and enthusiasm for good food. The interview went well and Mary was immediately offered the job. It seemed too good to be true – especially after she learnt that the salary was £1,000 a year, a large amount of money for a

22-year-old by anyone's standards back then. When she broke the news to her father Alleyne, he was dumbstruck. He couldn't believe her luck, especially after all her trials and tribulations at school – he'd assumed that perhaps Mary wouldn't find her feet in her career for years. So convinced was he that the offer from the Dutch Dairy Bureau wasn't all it was cracked up to be, he insisted on travelling from Bath to London to interview the firm himself to check that she wasn't lying and that the offer was genuine.

'That was my very first job after working for the Electricity Board in Bath, and I went to see this [gentleman] and he gave me the job and told me I would have a thousand a year,' Mary told *Desert Island Discs*. 'And I went back home, and my father looked at me, and he was on the next train the next day to see him. Anyway, he went and realised that it was all authentic.'

Alleyne returned home to Bath beaming with pride about his daughter's new-found success. Mary couldn't believe her luck either – she was astounded that she was finally going to be paid to carry out what she still regarded as a hobby. Every day Mary was expected to cook up milk-based recipes for the Dutch Dairy Bureau's numerous London-based clients. And at the end of each day, she could even take any leftovers home for her flatmates. It's fair to say that she excelled at the job. Mary was very hard-working for the Dutch Dairy Bureau – always on time for work, loved by bosses and given glowing appraisals.

But soon another, better job fell into Mary's lap. Staff at an on-the-up PR firm called Bensons were looking for a recipe tester to work for various clients they had on their books. Among many other clients, they represented Stork margarine, the egg and flour marketing boards and a farm called Eden Vale. To her delight, Mary applied and got the job. Her bosses at the Dutch Dairy Bureau couldn't recommend her highly enough and, although sad to see her go, she left for her new role with their best wishes. And the new job was even better than she could have imagined. 'I couldn't believe I was being paid to cook all day, every day, for everyone from the Egg Council to the Flour Advisory Board,' Mary has said. 'Being paid to do what I loved was a complete joy.'

Speaking about the specifics of the role, Mary said in an interview with the *Daily Mail*: 'I developed recipes, costed them out and had them photographed.' After years of struggling to find her forte, finally Mary felt that her life had a trajectory. Alleyne, who had previously been disappointed that his daughter had struggled in her academic studies, had developed a new respect for her.

'I used to go home every weekend,' says Mary. 'I didn't make my life in London. And I would drive up the drive and the door would open and Dad would have a gin and tonic [ready for me] and I would think I had arrived.' Finally Alleyne had realised that his daughter was starting to make a name for herself and was building up a well-deserved reputation.

For Mary, it was just the start of what would soon become an even more exciting career. Even today Mary says she's proud that both her parents were alive to witness the success she made of herself. Alleyne died aged 84 in 1993, while Margaret passed away peacefully in her sleep aged 105 on 24 May 2011, having seen her daughter become a celebrity off the back of her books and TV shows. Fittingly, considering what a big part Margaret had played in Bath's public life, a special service of thanksgiving was held at St Stephen's Church, Lansdown, in Bath, for the public – to 'celebrate an exceptional life', according to the death notice in the local newspaper. Mary and her brothers also held a private family funeral for their beloved mother. And for evermore Mary would credit her success to her parents. They were, she said, what had made the woman she would later become. 'I think that they were proud, and Mum particularly because she had all those years afterwards,' she told *Desert Island Discs*. 'But I think Dad was proud. But you see I was proud of my father. He achieved great things in Bath. So I am proud of him, and I think perhaps he was proud of me.' And speaking about her mother to the *Bath Chronicle*, Mary added: 'The secret to her long life, she would say, is to have patience, be pleasant to all around you, and enjoy what you have – not worry about what you haven't.' They were lessons in life that would live with Mary for some time.

But, at the start of her glittering career the sadness of her parents' deaths lay a long way in the future, and at the time Mary couldn't have been happier with her life in London. It was the late 1950s and the capital was an exciting place to live. The postwar boom was gathering pace and, after many years of rationing, the decade was proving to be a prosperous one. Growing affluence gave young Londoners a new assertiveness – they were inspired to live life to the full after the doom and gloom of the war. And, after years of soul-searching and wondering what to do with her life, Mary at last felt she had a place in the world as she went from strength to strength in her job at Bensons. She was one of the top-performing workers at the business and was thought of by the company's many influential clients as one of the best.

But despite being more than content with life, an exciting and unexpected career change was about to be thrust upon Mary – the opportunity to start writing for a woman's magazine called *Housewife*. This was to change the course of her professional life forever.

At the time, women's magazines were a booming trade. The 1950s was described as 'the golden age of women's magazine publishing' by Esther Walker in the *Independent*. Walker's article gives us an insight into the history of women's magazines through the years. At that time five out of six British women were said to have read at least one women's magazine a week – an incredible statistic that showed just how rapidly the market was growing. And while nowadays you might expect the latest female celebrity to adorn the cover, back in the 1950s, Walker says, if 'the front cover showed a picture of a happy woman holding a pie, it could sell as many copies as it could print'. Whereas today magazine editors might toil over catchy cover lines relating to showbiz, sex and style to reel readers in, the mere mention of cookery and homemaking was enough to captivate the stay-at-home mums of the 1950s.

While women's magazines were particularly flourishing in that era, they had a long and rich history dating back to the seventeenth century. The first to be published was the *Ladies' Mercury*. It was the brainchild of John Dunton, a professional bookseller who had edited the *Athenian Mercury*. Although the *Athenian Mercury* only published a few editions, it laid the ground for hundreds upon hundreds of other similar magazines. Printing technology during the

1700s and 1800s meant that it was impossible to illustrate the covers of magazines. But unlike today, there was no need to have a striking, eye-catching front cover in order to boost circulation, because the magazines weren't sold on newsstands. In fact, very rarely did any of them include pictures. The first to include an illustration was the June 1891 edition of *The Woman's Herald*, which included a drawing of a surly-looking Adeline Sergeant, a popular novelist at the time who often wrote about divine providence (and whose work has recently been given a new lease of life since being made available in the form of free e-books).

However, by the start of the 1900s, printing had developed to such a degree that all women's magazines could start to include colour illustrations. Walker said: 'Throughout the twenties and thirties, rather than today's lone cover girl, the front page often showed pictures of two or more people – sometimes a couple ice-skating.' To today's reader, it now seems that the more twee the cover image, the better a magazine sold. That image of a couple ice-skating was used on a cover of a January issue of the American edition of *Good Housekeeping*. That particular magazine became such a success stateside that it was brought to Britain in 1922 by the National Magazine Company. Understandably, there was a sea change in the approach to the content of women's magazines during the Second World War. Life became tough for women, many of whom were staying at home while their husbands were at war. As Walker said, magazines went from 'being a folly, however helpful, to being a true friend to women ... The challenges facing women were hard and unknown and the government used magazines as a way of communicating with the ever-more important home front.'

No longer did men feature on the front covers alongside women – now it was about having the woman standing by herself – independent, forthright and ready to take on the world. With their men at war, women were being forced to look out for themselves, and this was reflected in magazine covers of the time. On a 1945 cover of *Woman*, for example, a woman is seen plucking her eyebrows, or wearing an apron, or carrying corn, as was the case on the front cover of *My Home* from that same year.

As the postwar economy picked up and women became enchanted with the prospect of leading more exciting lives, the popularity of women's magazines continued to soar. Often they provided straightforward advice – with a large part of this dedicated to cookery. It was during the 1950s that magazines started to be sold on the newsstands. Prior to that, these magazines had predominantly been sold by subscription, with a few on sale in shops. The new development meant that editors had to find a way to encourage women who didn't know which magazine to pick to buy theirs – by using visually striking front covers packed with colour, and exciting taglines promising not-to-be-missed content. Walker notes that in one issue of *Home Chat* in 1955 cover lines were laid out with 'swooping lettering set at jaunty angles'. As long as women's magazines ticked certain boxes and fulfilled certain criteria, they would sell copies. Undoubtedly, one of those boxes was cookery – editors knew the importance of giving the subject due prominence in order to entice new readers. All women's magazines during this time dedicated a large chunk of their pages to cookery – as many still do today. Recipes, tips for creating the perfect Sunday lunch and 'agony aunt'-style columns in which experts answered readers' letters about problems they were having in the kitchen all featured heavily. Women would write in with queries about recipes and ask for help in choosing the best kitchen utensils.

It was against this backdrop that Mary was about to make an unexpected move into journalism. While she was still working at Bensons, the opportunity of some work came up at *Housewife* magazine, a popular title during the 1950s. The cookery editor had gone abroad, and the magazine needed cover for her position. Such was Bensons' reputation, the editor of *Housewife* contacted the firm to see if they had anyone suitable who could cover for the cookery editor. Immediately and without hesitation, Mary's boss recommended her.

Well, she didn't so much as recommend her, but instructed her that she would do it. 'While I was there, my boss said, "*Housewife*'s cookery editor has gone to Spain on a press trip and the pages aren't done. You will do it,"' Mary told *Desert Island Discs*.

Her insistence that Mary would take the work presented Mary with a dilemma. While it was an exciting development in her blossoming career, she knew full well how she had struggled with her studies at school. The words of her former school headmistress Miss Blackburn telling her she would never have a career rang in her ears. Mary was reluctant to take on the challenge and she made this known to her female boss.

'I said, I can cook, I can write recipes, but I can't do any more,' said Mary. 'I didn't pass English in my school cert.'

However, her boss came up with a solution. She told Mary to say the recipes out loud, as though she were talking someone through them in the kitchen. And as Mary said it out loud, she (the boss) would write the words Mary was saying down. It proved to be an ingenious technique … and one that lived on with Mary as she wrote over 70 cookbooks in the subsequent 50 years. '[My boss] said, you write the recipe as you talk to me,' Mary told *Desert Island Discs*. 'And I have always thought, I am chatting to the person who is doing the recipe.'

Bolstered by her boss's confidence, Mary realised the offer was too good to turn down and she agreed to go ahead with the assignment. Irrespective of her writing abilities, her passion for cooking shone through, and the simple, conversational style of her recipes was a hit with readers. No-nonsense and easy to follow, they were perfect for *Housewife* magazine. Very soon, the editors at *Housewife* were impressed by their new recruit and started to offer her work regularly whenever anything suitable arose.

As TV started to really take off during the 1960s, so the sales of women's magazines began to slide. The market had to modernise. Walker notes that in 1965, the publishing company IPC launched *Nova*, which was branded 'The new kind of magazine for a new kind of woman'. The front cover of the first issue was mostly black and highly stylised – the cover girl was reduced to a close-up image of a heavily made-up eye, and a large block of text proclaimed that *Nova* was a magazine that did things 'the 1965 way'. But although circulations may have not been what they once were, women's magazines still played a huge part in British journalism.

After years of working for *Housewife* on a part-time basis, Mary received a call. It was the editor of the magazine, with whom she had formed a good relationship over the years. The news was that there was a vacancy. The cookery editor had left to pursue other projects and they wanted to offer Mary the job. Despite having had initial reservations about getting involved with *Housewife* magazine, Mary had at that point been freelancing for them for some five years and she was thoroughly enjoying it – so she decided to take the plunge, leaving Bensons to take up a full-time role at *Housewife* in 1966. Mary spent four years there, becoming an integral part of the magazine as she ran the cookery section's recipes and columns single-handedly.

She then moved to *Ideal Home* magazine, into which *Housewife* was incorporated in 1970, and stayed there until 1973. The magazine's offices were based in central London. However, after marrying her husband Paul in 1966, Mary stopped living in London full-time and moved to the Buckinghamshire countryside where they set up their family home. Mary commuted to and from the capital on a daily basis, with the journey rarely taking more than an hour.

Ideal Home magazine went on to become one of the biggest in Britain. Today, *Ideal Home* is the UK's best-selling interiors magazine, with audited circulation figures for January to June 2012 sitting at just over 193,000 each month. The readership of the monthly magazine, meanwhile, was an impressive 1.035 million for the same period. The magazine's mantra today is that it has been 'empowering home-owners to make the most of their properties for over 80 years'. It had been launched in 1920, by the publishing company Odhams, as a direct rival to *Homes & Gardens*, published by their arch-enemies Newnes and launched in 1919. The magazine's first editor, Captain GC Clarke, said that *Ideal Home* aimed to strive against 'the erection of hideous houses which go to mar the beauty of what would under any other circumstances be the most ideal and beautiful environment'. This was a reference to the then government's promise, in 1921, to build 100,000 houses as part of its postwar planning. There was a general feeling that the government's attitude of building as many properties as quickly as possible would mean that design, comfort and ambience were being neglected. Despite the recent hardships of the war, families still wanted their homes to be enjoyable places in which to unwind, and this was why magazines such as *Ideal Home* became so hugely popular.

However, there was another reason why interior design magazines were being published in such abundance at the time. Following the end of the Great War, there had been a servant shortage. As a result, the middle classes, for the first time, had needed to learn how to run every aspect of their households, either totally by themselves or with very little and infrequent help. The launch of *Homes & Gardens* and *Ideal Home* and, later, the creation of a UK version of the popular US magazine *Good Housekeeping* in 1922, reflected these social changes and their impact on the market. *Ideal Home*, however, was undoubtedly leader of the pack and continued to supply interior decoration ideas for generations to come. Its popularity peaked in 1991, when it sold nearly half a million copies during the course of the year. Every issue includes a 20-page section dedicated to kitchen and bathroom makeovers. The emphasis is on simplicity and cost-effectiveness – features focus on easy ways for the readers to get the looks that adorn the pages of the magazine. Nowadays the magazine also includes articles on interior design, readers' homes, high-street shopping news and consumer advice. Sections such as the Savvy

Shopper buyers' guides help readers make informed choices when choosing key appliances, the latest technology, and major investments such as large pieces of furniture. Another regular feature is Simple Solutions, intended to make everyday life easier – from low-maintenance garden ideas to time-saving household tips. Over the years, the magazine has constantly tried to reinvent itself – for example, it underwent a design and content revamp with its May 2010 issue (which actually hit the newsstands at the end of March). It now sports new features, typography and layout along with a redesigned logo. Despite being primarily focused on interiors, the magazine's editors never lost sight of the importance of cookery's role in creating the sought-after domestic bliss, so recipes featured heavily – and this, of course, was Mary's remit.

As the popularity of cookery sections in magazines grew, so too did cookery books. Cookbooks were becoming big business during the late 1960s, as social and economic changes meant that servants and housemaids were less common, so more and more women were getting used to being self-sufficient in the kitchen. Housewives lapped up simple recipes that they could put together quickly for lunch with friends or for dinner once their husbands returned home from work, or increasingly, once they returned home from their own jobs. The emphasis was on traditional dishes that could be quickly put together at little cost.

At this point in history, cookery books in Britain had already had a long and rich history. To begin with, though, food was only ever one aspect covered by them. The author and journalist William Sitwell said: 'Mrs Beeton's late-nineteenth-century *Book of Household Management* was not novel in detailing everything from how to calculate your income tax, apply a bandage or deal with bad dreams alongside ideas for roly-poly jam pudding and veal olives. Thomas Dawson's *The Good Huswife's Jewell* of 1596 explains how "to restore speech that is lost suddenly" (you push a concoction of herbs up your nose) and includes an early diet plan – "For to make one slender" merely requires the brewing up of some fennel tea.'

However, for many decades after the First World War, cooking was an often tedious and dispiriting endeavour. As household help was scaled back, well-to-do women started to feel inseparable from the stove. Cooking became a necessity – rather than an activity to be enjoyed for its own sake. However, cookbooks played their part in turning this around. They showed women that spending time in the kitchen didn't have to be a chore, but could instead be a creative, enjoyable and enriching process. Cooking was gradually coming back into fashion. Sitwell noted: 'Women actually felt more chained to the kitchen than ever. Cooking became a drudgery and it took the likes of Elizabeth David, with her 1950 *A Book of Mediterranean Food*, to bring some glamour to the kitchen, celebrating delicious ingredients and the spirit of warmth from sunnier climes.' Developments in printing technology meant that producing full-colour, illustrated books with diagrams and photography became ever more economical, so cookery books evolved from the rather stark and bland tomes of the early twentieth century to more attractive objects. It became a pleasure to flick through for mealtime inspiration from the late 1970s onwards.

It was in this context that Mary was to make another,

unexpected, career move ... into the world of authoring cookbooks. This was to become the most significant moment in Mary's professional life to date – and one that would change the course of the rest of her adult life. As her reputation as a cookery journalist continued to grow, her name became well known among publishers. One publishing house, Hamlyn, was looking for their next big cookery writer, and Mary seemed like the perfect choice. She was unrivalled as one of the most-read and well-respected cookery journalists thanks to her time on both *Housewife* and *Ideal Home*. And so she seemed like the obvious choice to Hamlyn, to write what they wanted to be their definitive guide to easy-to-prepare, home-made recipes.

Mary admits she was delighted by the offer. To this day the book is 'one of her favourites', she said in an interview. It was quick to write, not least because Mary had many of the recipes to hand, having built them up over the years. The title, the publishers decided, would be simple, to be in keeping with the straightforward nature of the dishes. It would be called *The Hamlyn All Colour Cook Book*. And when Mary was handed her first copy, she admits that it was a significant moment for her. In an interview with the *Scotsman* she describes the publication of the book in 1970 as a 'turning point' in her life. No one could have anticipated the huge impact it would have. The book was hugely popular, and quickly found itself into homes up and down the country. In hardback it sold a staggering 1.5 million copies, and many more in paperback.

Its success came down to a few key factors. Mary's dishes, such as Dundee cake, duck à l'orange and black forest gateau, were very of the moment – perfect 1970s fare that all families could enjoy, without breaking the bank. The ingredients were all widely available in supermarkets or from the local grocer's. On a practical note, the layout of the book was also hugely appealing. There was a colour photograph for every recipe, something of a revolution in the early 1970s, when black and white snaps were still the norm. These photos made the book easy to navigate and allowed the cook using it to have something to aim for – the finished product was printed right there for them to see. If you got the dish right, you knew straight away.

The timelessness of Mary's first book has become apparent in recent years. Over the decades, it has been republished, updated and has had several editions. As Becky Sheaves wrote in the *Western Morning News* in 2010, the dishes now have a 'wonderfully retro-chic feel to them'. Indeed, some of the ingredients are rarely used, such as aspic – a gelatin made from meat stock – or consommé. Others have had to be modernised, like a lasagne that would need to be boiled for 10 minutes before being dished up. But regardless, cookery enthusiasts are still unwavering in their support for Mary's first book. One, Kathy Brown, wrote on online bookshop Amazon about the nostalgic effect of flicking through the book and how the recipes are still as relevant today as they were in the 1970s: 'We've had a copy of this in our house since I was a little girl in the 1970s. Mum was a keen cook and often made dishes from this book for dinner parties. I used to love leafing through the sections and looking at the lovely photographs. Eventually all of the members of our close family had a copy and so we'd turn up at each other's houses and recognise the dishes on the table. My grandmother, mother and aunts and uncles had a copy, and when mum and dad separated, Dad took the copy with him! I inherited my nan's copy when she died, and now my daughters cook from it. I will buy them each their own copy when they leave home. Favourites include Chilled Lemon Flan and Crunchy-topped Fish Pie. The recipes and ingredients are pretty retro (who makes syllabub these days?) and the measures are all imperial, but instructions are easy to follow and adapt, and even if your efforts don't turn out as spectacular as the ones in the photos, you'll quickly find family-favourite recipes of your own.'

The book's success turned Mary from a mere cookery editor into a best-selling author at the age of just 35. If ever she had needed a way to disprove her schoolteachers, then writing a best-selling cookery book was it! Mary couldn't believe her luck. She had always turned to cookbooks as she was growing up and discovering her love of cookery, especially while she was studying in Bath and Paris. In fact, there was one in particular that she would often use. 'My most-thumbed cookbook is Rosemary Hume's *Cordon Bleu Cookery*,' Mary told the BBC. 'When I first started out, having just qualified, that was my reference book; it's quite long-winded but it gave the correct method.'

But never could Mary have imagined in her wildest dreams that she herself would be penning a cookbook one day. And while Mary may have been surprised to be offered a book deal at first, given her self-confessed reluctance to engage at school, publishers were about to start clambering all over each other to sign her up to do other books. She quickly became one of the most celebrated cookery writers in Britain. Often described as a 'pioneer', she built her success on combining large sales figures with being published frequently

– on more than one occasion she released two books in the space of a year. To date she has published more than 70 books, selling in excess of 5 million copies. And it seemed there was also demand for Mary's recipes abroad. Some of her books were translated into other languages, making her a star away from the UK as well. Two were translated into French – *Délicieux desserts* and *La vraie pâtisserie toute simple* – and sold well throughout France. Meanwhile, Mary also had her recipes translated into Spanish. *Guia Básica De Las Tecnicas Culinarias* was released in 1998.

The range of books Mary has written is almost as impressive as the numbers they've sold. She provided quick and easy recipes for people leading busy lives in *Real Fast Food* and *Day by Day Cooking*. Her love of baking and cake making is a constant theme in her oeuvre – including in *My Kitchen Table: 100 Cakes and Bakes*, *Fast Desserts* and *Glorious Puds*. Others were written to tie in with her TV series, while some were more left-field. *Food as Presents* was, as the title suggests, an interesting take on combining cooking with gift giving for Christmas, birthdays and anniversaries. And though her output became prolific, Mary always made sure that the books were written to the highest possible standard and would constantly check over the recipes before the books went to press, poring over the proofs to make sure they were perfect and nothing was wrong. 'I've developed something of an obsession with accuracy and detail,' she admitted in an interview with the *Scotsman*. Later, she teamed up with her long-time assistant Lucy Young. Young regularly helped her with the research and writing of the books, particularly as Mary's schedule became increasingly busy. Years later they went on to co-author some cookery books together, and Lucy wrote her own collection, which sold just as well as Mary's.

Meanwhile, Mary's journalism career was going from strength to strength, as cookery editors rushed to sign her up to write regular columns for their publications. She would later contribute recipes regularly to the *Daily Telegraph* newspaper and the *Daily Mail* website which, like most things Mary writes, became especially popular because of the way she often peppered the recipes with anecdotes and advice, in the conversational tone she had used since her first recipes for *Housewife*. For example, in her Chocolate and Vanilla Marble Loaf recipe she said: 'This loaf cake looks spectacular and is lovely for a special occasion.' And while writing about her Devonshire scones recipe she added: 'The secret to good scones is not to handle them too much before baking, and to make the mixture on the wet, sticky side.' The beauty of Mary's recipes, it seems, comes down to her presence in them. Mary's love of cooking never seemed far from her written work.

Aside from national newspapers, Mary embraced the chance to write for more niche magazines over the years, too. Practicality has always been paramount for Mary in her approach to cooking, and just as she blazed a trail for new cooking technology when employed by Bath Electricity Board, she has long been an advocate of the benefits of freezing. She's often seen as the first high-profile cook to espouse the joys of freezing food, while others were turning their noses up at the practice. As a result, Mary gave regular tips and advice about freezing in *Freezer Monthly* magazine, and even wrote one of her first books on the theme – *Popular Freezer Cookery*. Years later, in 1985, Mary published the

Iceland Guide to Cooking from Your Freezer, in conjunction with the popular high-street supermarket, a deal she doubtless secured as 'Brand Mary', became increasingly well known as a reliable and authoritative voice in the world of cooking. Mary's mantra in her books was always the same – from *The Hamlyn All Colour Cook Book* to the recipe books that were released off the back of the *Great British Bake Off*: keep it simple. The beauty of her recipes, it seems, is that they are straightforward and don't over-complicate the sometimes tricky process of cooking. Not only does Mary try to keep the process user-friendly, but she constantly strives to keep the ingredients she uses in her recipe books as unpretentious as possible. It's doubtless one of the reasons they have become so successful over the years. 'I think that nowadays we're in danger of making cooking and entertaining too complicated, which makes it stressful,' Mary said in an interview with the *Scotsman*. 'I always use food in season and, before I decide what to cook, I have a look in my garden to see what's growing and then plan my meal around that. For wholesome, enjoyable food there's no need for a huge list of ingredients, so my store cupboard has remarkably few herbs and spices.'

Her prolific output when it comes to her cookery books has been a lesson in itself for Mary. She is in the unique position of having written books in five separate decades. It gives her a level of insight that few other cookery writers today enjoy. With more than 60 years of experience in cookery, she says there's one clear thing that has changed during this period. She told the *World of Books* blog: 'I think it's the ingredients – they are more readily available, and basic ingredients are more prepared. In the 1960s chicken breasts did not exist – you had to buy a chicken, cut it in four and use the breasts, legs, wings and drumsticks.' Mary also admits that attitudes to health and diet have affected the kinds of recipes that she uses in her cookbooks these days. 'We use less fat nowadays, too, less sugar and non-stick pans,' she told the website. 'The choice of dairy has changed too, with crème fraîche, mascarpone and lots of different creams available, which means icings for cakes do not always need to be the same.' As with *The Hamlyn All Colour Cook Book*, Mary's books have often had to be revised because of these changing trends over the years. Her *Complete Cookbook* was re-released years later as *Mary Berry's Complete Cookbook,* with an extra 30 new recipes, including some customised for dinner parties that took on board changes in tastes and the availability of ingredients and kitchen utensils. Coming up with new ideas for answering that age-old question of 'what's for dinner tonight, Mum?' has become part of Mary's day-to-day job. 'Luckily we get new ingredients all the time, and they become popular and fashionable: fennel, red chard, new salad leaves,' she told the website. 'I am now revisiting classic recipes from the 1970s. My assistants Lucy and Lucinda are young, and give me new ideas like bowl food, risottos, wraps ...'

Her dedication to her cookery-book writing and her constant desire to be original resulted in Mary being voted into the top three of the most trusted cookery writers, alongside Jamie Oliver and Delia Smith. 'That was a huge accolade, I must admit,' she told the *Western Morning News*, in her typically modest fashion. Mary is someone whose recipes can be relied on time and time again, and so the award was perhaps expected by those who have followed her career. However, over the years, she has received a seemingly endless stream of letters from fans of her books who, nevertheless, can't quite seem to get the hang of her recipes. Never one to put the boot in, Mary is diplomatic in the way she handles such criticism. 'I get emails from people saying I tried such and such a recipe and my cake went down in the middle,' she told the *Daily Telegraph*. 'They never think it might be them, or their oven.'

Her popularity as an author means that Mary often travels the country to take part in book signings, and on these days it's not unusual for queues to be seen snaking around the book section at large, prestigious department stores such as Selfridges in London. Writing books, it seems, has become a passion for Mary, not just a career – it's something she cherishes and is as thankful for as she is all the other work that she does. Spending time with her fans and talking to them seems an enjoyable process for Mary, rather than a chore. She hopes that in years to come, cookery enthusiasts will still be thumbing through her recipe books, even as the popularity of devices such as the iPad and Kindle and other e-book readers increases. 'I love the touch of a book and the passing through the family generations, and [even] recycling them,' she told the *World of Books* website. 'Hopefully there is a place for both books and e-books in the future.'

But the irony of becoming such a well-respected author is not lost on Mary. As a young girl, she could never have imagined this outcome, when she struggled so much with her English studies while at school. So when it comes to her recipe for success, Mary has joked in the past – in a typically self-deprecating manner – that she couldn't do it without the help of a good editor. Asked by Kirsty Young about the seeming disparity between her failure to make the grade at English in her school cert, and the fact that she would later publish so many books, Mary quipped: 'The spelling is pretty bad.'

But as well as her huge collection of books, there was another way in which Mary was able to teach the public the joys of cookery and baking. As Mary became the doyenne of British baking, her loyal fans didn't just want to read her books – they wanted to see her whipping up her recipes and extolling her advice in person. Her numerous TV appearances were one way of allowing this to happen. But in between, when Mary's series have been off air, there has been an alternative way in which her legions of followers could see her – at the scores of cookery demonstrations she still performs at a vast number of venues across the UK. Often they are for small groups of people or as part of a charity fundraiser. On other occasions they have been part of a big food festival. Usually these demonstrations involve Mary producing a handful of her best-loved recipes for the eager onlookers. Sometimes the audience can get involved in the baking process themselves and follow along with Mary as she cooks. A tasting session may be part of the event, as well as the opportunity to pick Mary's brain for advice and help in the kitchen during the course of a question and answer session. At the demonstrations Mary's always happy to sign copies of her books for her fans too, and is often besieged at the end by attendees desperate for a signature. At one point Mary was carrying out a staggering 30 demonstrations a year – more than one every fortnight. These have seen her travel the length and breadth of the country. As they became more frequent, Mary's PA Lucy would often have to help with the organizational side of things, and would regularly get involved with assisting during the demonstrations, too. As far as Mary's concerned, the cooking demonstrations have been a great way of adding variety to her working life. 'It's so nice to have a job where one day I might be doing a demonstration, another I'm at home writing recipes and another I'm teaching,' she said in one interview. 'It's such good fun.'

The biggest cookery demonstration that Mary attends regularly was the BBC Good Food Show. Now held four times a year, in London, Glasgow and at Birmingham's NEC, it's the UK's biggest food show. A spin-off show was also held at the Bluewater shopping centre in Kent in April 2012, so popular have they become over the decades. Showcasing a huge variety of different culinary delights, the shows often see more than 40 chefs, celebrities and food experts descend on the conference centre for the five-day-long show. In total there are often more than 200 demonstrations during the course of the exhibition. Mary has attended the show for years, demonstrating a huge range of her favourite recipes. And after she had been a regular for decades, in 2012, for the first time, the Good Food Show included a *Great British Bake Off* stage. This was a testament to how big the show had become after its third series, which saw ratings reach a 6.5 million peak as *Bake Off* fever gripped the nation. Not only were Mary and her co-judge Paul Hollywood featured on the stage, but so too were other familiar faces from the show, carrying out a string of demonstrations for visitors looking for exciting baking recipes for the festive season. The winner of series three, John Whaite, made his first live debut after being crowned in first place. Alongside John Whaite was Joanne Wheatley, who had triumphed in the second series of the show. She kept the crowds entertained with some of her own recipes from the cookbook she released in the aftermath of winning the show. The *Great British Bake Off* stage also welcomed the renowned cake sculpturist Connie Viney, who had also delighted fans of the show. Other stages at the Good Food Show featured other popular cookery programmes, such as *MasterChef* and *Saturday Kitchen Live*.

But for Mary, having carried out demonstrations to small groups of people over the years, the fact that she now had her own stage off the back of one of her programmes, at such a highly reputed show, demonstrated just how far her career had come. Mary says that while she loves carrying out these demonstrations, she isn't a fan of taking her work home with her. She admits she often gets a little put out if friends or family insist on her performing private demonstrations in her own kitchen. 'I love doing workshop demonstrations,' Mary said in an interview with the *Daily Telegraph*. 'But I hate it when friends and family hover over me and say, "Let's see how you're meant to make gravy." I feel as though I'm being judged, so I usually ask them to leave me to it.' And while her friends and family may have to go without learning directly from Mary, millions of others continue to do so. With her many cookbooks, and tickets to her cookery demonstrations selling like hot cakes even to this day, Mary has been able to impart her incredible wealth of baking knowledge to a huge number of people. And with more books and demonstrations in the pipeline, that looks set to carry on for the foreseeable future.

CHAPTER 4

FAMILY MATTERS

As Mary's journalism career started to take off, so too did her love life. In 1964, two years before she joined *Housewife* full-time, she met Paul Hunning. Although she may not have realised it at the time, their relationship would go on to be one of the most – if not *the* most – significant in her life. She was introduced to Paul – a dealer in antiquarian books and paintings – through one of her brothers, and they started dating. In 1966, the same year she started at *Housewife* magazine, they married, when Mary was 30 years old.

Mary remembers the first years of their relationship with affection. In fact, she goes as far as to say that during the course of 45 years of marriage their love has grown even deeper. She never took his name professionally, but this is no reflection on the depth of her devotion.

'I met my husband Paul in 1964,' she recalled in an interview with *Desert Island Discs* in 2012. 'He was a friend of my brother's. We got married in 1966 and have just celebrated our 45th anniversary. I love him even more now than I did when I married him.'

While Mary's focus on her career earned her the admiration of her colleagues, her work life by no means came before her marriage. In many respects, Mary and Paul had a very traditional marriage – with both of them taking on quite stereotypical roles at home. Not surprisingly, it's Mary who runs the kitchen, as Paul struggles with even the minutest of domestic tasks.

'I know I spoil him rotten,' Mary said. 'My sister-in-law once visited while I was away working; she asked for a cup of tea and Paul didn't know where the tea was or how to make it. It's my fault because I've never encouraged him. Paul and I never shout at each other. To argue with my husband upsets me so much that it's not worth it.'

Soon after they married, Mary and Paul moved out of London for a slightly quieter life in Buckinghamshire. This meant that Mary could continue to commute easily to London for work, but the location felt more appropriate to them to start a family, which they would soon do. After spending some time searching for properties, eventually they settled on a house called Watercroft in the village of Penn. They still live there today, and it was there that Mary would bring up her family, write some of her best-selling books, mastermind her businesses, entertain hundreds of people at dinner parties and run the first of her now-famous Aga cookery classes.

An online history website gives a run-down of Watercroft's past owners. The house itself is steeped in a rich history. Watercroft was a farm that had been previously owned by the

Grove dynasty, a large landed-gentry family whose association with Penn dates back to the 1300s. According to an online family tree, Watercroft was a farm when occupied by Thomas Blades Grove, the elder brother of Sir George Grove, both grandsons of Yeoman Grove, at the end of the nineteenth century. Twenty-eight years earlier John Grove, Yeoman Grove's fifth son, the fishmonger of the village's New Bond Street, had died there, in 1868. Believed to be a Queen Anne house, it has not been greatly altered and still has the original front door and interior panelling. The upper storey has wrought-iron balconies to the windows. It has a large, beautiful garden surrounded by a high wall, which Mary and Paul would put to good use. The dovecote – a structure for housing doves and pigeons – had originally been a brewery, many years previously. Articles on the Internet suggest that the ownership of the house passed from Thomas Blades Grove, who died there on 9 November 1897, to Sir George Grove, the music writer who became acclaimed as the founding editor of *Grove's Dictionary of Music and Musicians*. It continued to be passed down through the generations, coming eventually to Edmund and Sheila Grove. During the Second World War, Edmund served in the army, and was killed in action in 1940. A Mr Kann wanted to buy Watercroft from Sheila, but she was so emotionally invested in the property she would only lease it to him to begin with, as she struggled to come to terms with the death of her husband. However, Mr Kann and his wife Joycie succeeded in buying it from her in 1953. Mary and Paul bought the property from the Kanns and have lived there ever since. Mary would even come to name some of her recipes after the property, including Watercroft Flaky Cheese Biscuits and Watercroft Whipped Potatoes.

Both Mary and Paul became keen gardeners once they moved to Watercroft. Aside from her time in the kitchen, Mary would spend hours tending to their garden at Watercroft, which is made up of three sprawling acres, with beautiful views over the Chilterns. It became the focal point of the property, and Mary and Paul even open it to the public under the National Gardens Scheme, so anyone can enjoy it by paying a small entry fee of £3.50. According to local leaflets, some of the highlights include the garden's rose walk, which includes lots of seating areas, summer pots and the herb and vegetable garden. There's also a natural pond complete with wildlife, and a wildflower meadow as well. During the summer months, the Berrys lay on afternoon teas and occasionally a prize raffle as well, and one year called in an unusual favour from the local branch of the supermarket Waitrose: 'Once we opened our garden for the National Gardens Scheme and I made masses of scones. There was no way I could put them all in the freezer, so I nipped down there and asked, "Do you mind keeping a couple of big bags for me and I'll pick them up on Sunday morning?" and they said it was no problem. It's lovely.'

In an interview with the *Daily Telegraph*, Mary spoke about how the kitchen and garden provide her with hours of relaxation – and plenty of work: 'This old trug always sits in the kitchen so I can nip out to the garden and pick flowers or herbs whenever I choose. We have two gardeners, Kevin and Simon, but I choose all the plants and muck in whenever I'm at home. We've just introduced an arch of pears, but the roses are the real feature. My favourite, Chandos Beauty, won first prize in our village show this year.'

Mary has often spoken enthusiastically about her love of

gardening, which appears to be second only to her love of cooking. 'I absolutely must have big bunches of fresh, seasonal flowers dotted around the house,' she told the *Daily Express*. 'Paul and I are both passionate gardeners and we always make sure we have something growing all year round, even in the depths of winter. This morning I've been into my garden and picked a lovely bunch of jasmine and winter honeysuckle. I always keep a huge selection of paper and ribbons in the kitchen to make up bouquets of flowers from my garden for friends and family.'

In other interviews Mary has gone into more depth about what she loves to grow in the gardens at Watercroft. 'I grow parsley in rows, mixing the seeds of the moss-curled and flat-leaf varieties together,' she told the *Daily Telegraph*. 'I pour boiling water on the drill pre-sowing and have no germination problems. I have tried many plants, including bougainvilleas, but the pelargoniums are perfect. All they need is deadheading, feeding and watering and they always look amazing. Rocket is a magnet for flea beetle, but sow after August and you will avoid having leaves peppered with their minuscule holes.' She told the *Financial Times*: 'In the garden we grow what we enjoy most. As it's winter, we have a few leeks, and that's about it. In spring we'll have salads, spring onions, carrots, a few strawberries; we don't grow any brassicas because the pigeons would get them. We're fairly fortunate with rabbits.'

Above all else, Watercroft became a retreat for her and Paul from their busy lives. As Mary's work schedule has become more and more hectic, she clearly finds returning to Watercroft a relaxing experience after a long day. Normally, if she's filming, despite her age Mary is up at 5am and then not home before 7pm. But if she's not working, like any other married couple, Mary and Paul have a set routine that they rarely waver from.

'Paul gets up first and I have a little lie-in while he shaves,' said Mary to the *Daily Telegraph*. 'Then, while he takes our labrador, Millie, for a walk, I empty the dishwasher, put the dog food out and plan our evening meal. Breakfast is always toast and Marmite. If I'm not filming, I spend the morning testing recipes for my latest cookbook with my assistant, Lucy. In the afternoon I may go out with Paul to buy plants, and then it's time to prepare supper. Paul's favourite is fish pie with smoked haddock, served with cooked cubes of potato and white sauce flavoured with mustard and lemon, topped with cheese. We usually have vegetables from the garden, though after this year's bumper crop I never want to see another runner bean as long as I live!'

Such is Mary's interest in gardening that she admitted to the BBC how, should Paul not be available to join her at a dream dinner, her alternative dining partner would be a gardener: 'My husband, of course, but otherwise Monty Don. I'm a great gardener, and now he's returned to *Gardeners' World*, I watch it avidly. He's so relaxed; and he always reminds me of all the jobs I ought to be doing over the weekend.'

As well as cooking and gardening, Mary and Paul try very hard to keep as active as possible, despite both of them being well into their seventies. In particular Mary enjoys playing tennis, even today, as well as regularly going for long walks. 'I hate gyms,' said Mary in an interview with the *Scotsman*. 'The whole thought of being cooped up, pedalling a bike or on a running machine, appals me. For me, a once-weekly morning of not-serious tennis is what I love, as well as plenty of gardening and walks with the dogs.' Millie and Coco are important members of the Berry household, and are taken on long walks by Mary and Paul in the Buckinghamshire countryside surrounding Watercroft.

With her usual modesty, Mary insists she's not the world's best tennis player, even though she always makes time to play with her friends ... once they have exchanged gossip and caught up.

'I've been playing tennis with the same three friends for 20 years and it means a lot to me,' she said to the *Daily Telegraph*. 'They arrive at 10 o'clock every Monday morning, but an hour later Paul will walk into the kitchen and say, "Have you had a good game?" and we'll still be drinking coffee. My standard isn't high, but at my age you have to keep fit. I'd hate people to see me huge and say, "Oh, that's because she eats so much cake."'

Indeed, despite being such a champion of cake baking, Mary hates the thought of leading an unhealthy lifestyle. As well as staying active, she always makes sure that she and Paul eat a balanced diet.

'I think moderation is the key,' she has said. 'So I eat healthily, a little of everything: meat, fish, butter, cream and lots of fruit and vegetables. No in-between-meal snacks, but I always say "yes" to strawberries with cream, a piece of cake on Sundays and a large glass of wine every day!'

And despite having been together for so long, the couple rarely argue. You might imagine that, like most other couples, Mary and Paul would have the odd tiff. But Mary says that one of the last pieces of worldly wisdom her father Alleyne imparted to her before his death was to avoid fighting at all costs. 'Never let a day end with a quarrel,' Mary once said in an interview. 'This was the advice given to Paul, my husband, on our wedding day by my father. We gave the same advice to our son and daughter before they got married, because it has stood us in such good stead. After all, arguments often start at the end of the day when you're doing chores and you're tired, so why lose sleep over something that you realise doesn't even matter in the morning?'

While appearances on TV and radio would go on to form a large part of Mary's career, she admits she's also partial to watching or listening with a cup of tea and slice of cake on the sofa when she has a spare moment. 'Over the years there have been a few choice radio and television programmes that have enriched my life, or at least made a quiet night in more enjoyable,' she said in an interview. 'In the week, the moment I'm in the car it is Radio 4. The *Today* programme, *Woman's Hour* or a good play all help the drive go by. Oh how I miss *The Forsyte Saga* and more recently *Monarch of the Glen*, but with any luck it's *Heartbeat* – which always has a happy ending!'

After settling at Watercroft, it wasn't long before Mary and Paul decided they wanted to start a family. And they didn't delay – having three children in the space of four years. At the age of 30, Mary was already considered relatively old to be having her first child and so it made sense that she wasted no time in having more children. First came Thomas, followed by a daughter, Annabel, and finally William. Her stable family life surrounded by her husband and three children brought Mary a sense of happiness. Asked in an interview with the women's magazine *The Lady* what the most fulfilling moment of her life was, Mary said: 'When Paul, my husband, and I had our third child. We had two boys and a girl and I just thought "Gosh, we're a family now."' Finally, life felt complete for Mary.

But as important as her home life was to Mary, she never forgot how hard she had worked to build up her career. It had been a hard slog for her to make her mark on the cookery world and, as a result, she rarely took time off work – even after she had given birth. In fact, after having each baby she only ever took five weeks off work from the magazine. Such a thing in this day and age is practically unheard of. Nowadays in the UK, female employees are entitled to 52 weeks of maternity leave, 39 weeks of which is paid, planned to rise to 52 weeks paid, with the first six weeks paid at 90 per cent of full pay. The remainder is at a fixed rate, which was £135.45 a week as of 2012. Most employers offer a more generous policy and annual leave continues to accrue throughout the maternity leave period.

But it wasn't always as good. At the time Mary had her children, the concept of maternity leave simply did not exist, as she has often recalled in interviews. The issue of women taking time off after giving birth was first put on the political agenda in 1911, following the National Insurance Act which was proposed by the then Chancellor David Lloyd George. It was the first time universal maternal health benefit was introduced, and as a result, debates started to be had about the rights of new mums. By 1941, women were being conscripted into industry. The issue of 'double burden' – the fact that women were both having to work and being expected to look after the children – started to be considered.

Within two years, 1,345 nurseries had been established, whereas in 1940 there had been just 14. This enabled women to work by getting help looking after the children. During the 1950s, 1960s and 1970s, when Mary was establishing herself professionally, maternity leave was still not on the agenda, although it was becoming a serious issue by 1974, after Sweden introduced a law on parental leave. By the 1980s, maternity leave varied from company to company and would depend on how long you had worked for the firm. A landmark case in 1987 appeared to show that mothers' rights were being curbed when training supervisor Maria Brown lost a lawsuit against her employer after she was made redundant because she was pregnant. But a sea change came about in 1999 after New Labour swept into power. The introduction of the Employment Relations Act meant all employees were given a minimum of three months' unpaid parents' leave and mothers were entitled to 18 weeks of paid leave.

When Mary gave birth to her children it was a different story. With no fixed system in place, Mary was determined not to leave behind the career she had worked so hard for. 'I didn't give up work at all. The maternity "leave" wasn't really – you were really expected to leave and not come back,' she says. 'Well I so enjoyed what I did I came back very soon and didn't have a smart nanny either.' While at home Mary was always in charge in the kitchen, but Paul helped out when it came to making sure the kids got to school on time. 'None of my friends had careers, but I loved my work and Paul was marvellous with things like the school run,' said Mary. 'It wasn't like today. If you didn't come back to your job soon, someone else would jump into your shoes.

By then, I was cooking editor of a magazine and there was lots of competition.'

Much like Mary's own childhood, she and Paul made sure their own kids had a pretty idyllic life. In a lot of ways it was similar to the life Mary had growing up in Bath. Mary admits she was conscious that she wanted them to have the same experiences that she had. 'When the children were young we very much had an outdoor life,' she said. 'They were all very sporty. And really, you had to keep them busy.' Also, like their mother, the three much preferred their outdoor adventures to being bookish. None of them, it seemed, enjoyed the written word at a young age, just as Mary hadn't when she was a youngster. 'They were not the ones who were sitting in a corner with a book, none of them, with a book and their knees up in front of them,' said Mary. 'They were out playing and getting into trouble.'

That outdoors existence was obviously something that had a deep impact on Mary's oldest child, Tom. As he grew older, he turned it into a career and became a tree surgeon, eventually setting up his own business, called Penn Tree Services. Based near Watercroft in High Wycombe, Buckinghamshire, and established in 1996, the business is based at Tom's family home. He later married Sarah and they went on to have twin girls – Abby and Grace – the first two of Mary's grandchildren.

Tom has, by and large, avoided being in the limelight as a result of being one of Mary's offspring. But Mary's daughter Annabel wasn't so shy, and she went on to contribute a lot to her mother's career. Following in her mother's footsteps, she too trained at Le Cordon Bleu in Paris before returning to the UK. She had a brief stint at The London College of Fashion and afterwards took up a short placement at *Vogue* magazine. Unsure about exactly what she wanted to do with her life, Annabel moved to the island of Bali, Indonesia, where she set up her own fashion label called Venus Rising. Spurred on by its success, Annabel decided she wanted to return to the UK and try her hand at running a business there. Aged 19, she set up Cosmetic Candles in London, with help from a grant from The Princes Trust, the Prince of Wales' charity that helps get youngsters a head-start in life. It was a hard slog to make the business a success, and this involved Annabel travelling around the country on a shoestring to sell her products wherever possible. It certainly wasn't the glamorous life she might have become used to while at *Vogue*. She said, in an interview for the official Mary Berry website: 'I had a VW camper and used to go around the country selling the candles at shows and festivals.' Annabel's early wanderlust is not something Mary shares, as she confided to the *Daily Express*. Despite loving the hot sunshine of an English summer, she's so settled among family and friends that upping sticks for anywhere else is not a tempting prospect: 'Yet as much as I love to be warm, I have never been tempted to move somewhere sunnier. Britain is my home and I really couldn't imagine living anywhere else.'

By 1991, Mary's career was becoming ever busier. On top of the cookery books, her TV and radio work was taking off. She was in demand all the time. As she continued to juggle her home and work life, Paul came up with a suggestion that would be potentially lucrative – to bottle the home-made sauces and salad dressings she made for their meals at home and sell them. It seemed like a brilliant idea, and none of her family could fathom why they hadn't thought of it sooner.

With her media work becoming more and more frequent and high profile, Mary was beginning to understand the power of her name. She had a legion of loyal fans who read her recipes and books, and would eagerly present her with examples of their own baking whenever she went to speak at a charity event. So it was logical to use that name to promote her businesses and reach an even wider audience. She may have struggled with maths at school, but there is no denying that Mary is a canny businesswoman, heading an empire that has spanned books, television and, later, a cookery school. Now, as well as seeing her name on the spines along a bookshelf, Paul had presented an idea that would see 'Mary Berry' become a familiar name in the supermarket aisles as well.

She was a pioneer in this way. No cook had really successfully transitioned from writing cookbooks to having products bearing their name at that time. Mary really became the first cook to use her name to build a business empire that would become far bigger than her cookbooks – not that she realised this at the time.

To begin with, however, Mary had little time to devote to this new enterprise. But Annabel, with her entrepreneurial streak, saw the opportunity to create a successful business. She said '[Mum] was very busy ... But she thought it was a great idea and told me to go ahead.' She seized the chance to get involved.

There was another reason why Annabel was so enthused by the idea. She had grown up eating her mother's sauces and dressings. She knew the products inside out and she even admitted in one interview that when she was little she couldn't eat anything unless she had some of her mother's trusty salad dressing on the dinner table. 'Since I was a toddler, I have been addicted to it!' she said. 'I remember when I was five, we were in our VW camper in France and I wouldn't eat any food because Mum forgot her salad dressing. She bought the ingredients and we shook it in an old bottle and I drank it.'

Her love for her mother's recipe was reflected in her determination and dedication to move it from their kitchen table on to the tables of millions around the country. And so Annabel set about creating the business from nothing through sheer hard graft. There were no big investors or backing from supermarket chains in those days. Selling food products off the back of a cook's name alone was an unknown quantity and no one knew how successful it would be. So Annabel quite literally built the business with her own hands. In 1994 she saved £100 in cash, before heading to a market in the East End of London, where she bought some old-fashioned bottles with corks in. Next, she made up a batch of salad dressing. 'I drew flowers on the labels and called it Mary Berry's Original Family Recipe Salad Dressing,' Annabel said. 'Then I tied the label around the neck of the bottle with string and sticky tape!' Then aged 21, Annabel travelled the country just as she had done with Cosmetic Candles, and started selling the sauces and dressings at up to 40 agricultural shows a year. 'I started selling the dressing at shows, festivals ... Then in 1994, the range was launched and branded "Mary Berry & Daughter",' recalled Annabel. Original Family Recipe Salad Dressing was quickly followed by Mary Berry's Special Mustard Dressing.

Demand for the products, which were then sold at Mary's Aga Workshops, was so high that they decided they needed to expand. The company quickly progressed, landing a contract with kitchenware chain Lakeland, and soon their products were being distributed nationwide. The range was launched in supermarkets across the country, and eventually in Ireland and Germany as well – and they can still boast that they are the UK's leading provider of gourmet salad dressings and sauces. And it didn't stop there. Annabel continued to develop more products from her mother's recipes, and the range today includes Caesar Dressing, three unique chutneys and an Oriental Sauce. In 2008, a fine food distributor called RH Amar bought a minority stake in the brand, whose annual sales were worth £3 million. From £100 cash, Annabel had managed to create a multi-million-pound business.

But aside from Annabel's hard work, it became clear that there was another reason why people were so keen to snap up Mary's products. It was soon evident that shoppers knew they could expect the best when they saw Mary's name on the label. And, typically, her sauces have become kitchen wonders. The dressings are mostly used for salads but are also popular as a spread for sandwiches instead of butter and as a sauce for pasta. The sauces can also be used for marinating, basting and dipping. They can even be used for adding flavour to stir-fries and glazing meat before roasting.

And in 2011, with perfect timing for capitalising on her *GBBO* success, Mary Berry & Daughter launched a range of cake mixes for time-poor cooks wanting to bake quality cakes. Sold in Waitrose supermarkets, the range includes Lemon Drizzle, Luxury Carrot Cake and Double Chocolate Fudge, packaged up in a disposable tray to bake the cake in. Food snobs have sometimes suggested that using a cake mix isn't the 'proper way' to go about knocking up a sweet treat in the kitchen. But Mary is defiant, and insists that it simply helps get more people baking who otherwise wouldn't have done.

'It's all about encouraging people to have a go. You just add eggs and butter,' Mary told the *Western Morning News*. 'There is nothing nicer than a cake straight from the oven, after all.'

With her range of branded products, Mary was in many ways a trailblazer. Many cooks have followed in her footsteps, but she was the first cook to use her name as a merchandising tool to reach as many fans as possible. Similarly, younger celebrity cooks such as Jamie Oliver and Nigella Lawson have endorsed kitchen equipment and ingredients in recent years as they encourage more of us to try home cooking – after all, who is better placed to recommend a product than a professional who spends hundreds of hours a year creating new recipes? But they would be hard pressed to match Mary's record of cookbook writing. And with Mary's pioneering business model to look at, they have been able to build their empires in a much shorter timeframe. Unlike Mary, they all seem to have an alter ego as the starting point for their brand. Jamie Oliver was initially known as the Naked Chef thanks to his cockney accent, relaxed appearance and no-nonsense attitude in the kitchen, where he's often happy to eschew strict weights or measurements in his recipes. Meanwhile, Nigella is the self-styled Domestic Goddess, whose tendency to wear figure-hugging outfits that enhance her enviable curves while she concocts gooey desserts has been the subject of hundreds of column inches from TV reviewers. They are brands too, following in Mary's footsteps by seeing the potential to capitalise on their name, while giving TV viewers the confidence to cook their dishes at home.

Jamie Oliver, 40 years Mary's junior, is following a similar template to hers in terms of mapping out his brand, with a range that includes seasonings, pasta sauces and stuffings. Revenue from his books has allowed him to provide a comfortable home life for his wife, Jools, and their young family. Where Mary had her Aga Workshops, Jamie set up Fifteen, a restaurant run by apprentices who want to move away from their difficult backgrounds through what Jamie calls 'meaningful hard work'. Such has been the success of the London training scheme and restaurant, there are now branches of Fifteen in Cornwall and Amsterdam, too. On top of that, he's fought for a new approach to healthy eating in schools in a campaign that took him all the way to Downing Street and eventually earned him an MBE. It was a campaign that may not have gained so much momentum if his profile wasn't already so high, and his brand wasn't so popular and trusted.

Mary is a huge fan of Jamie, telling Kirsty Young on *Desert Island Discs* that she thought him 'absolutely brilliant' for his attempts to bring real cooking back into schools. 'Cooking should be in school. When everybody leaves school, whether they are boys or girls, what do they have to do in the home? Produce a meal. And they haven't been taught to do it. I think it should be absolutely essential,' she said. Mary admits to keeping an eye on her successors on TV: 'I like watching Rick Stein ... Jamie Oliver is lovely, too, and Hugh Fearnley-Whittingstall has made us all think about the fish we eat. But chefs like Gordon Ramsay ... well, I suppose people like it, but I can do without the ranting,' she told the *Daily Mail*.

Another celebrity cook who has trodden a similar branding path as Mary is Nigella Lawson. Her success also means that her brand is instantly recognisable to any fan of her TV series, just with the utterance of her first name. Her first cookbook, *How to Eat*, sold 300,000 copies and became a best-seller. Two years later *How to be a Domestic Goddess* won her a British Book Award for Author of the Year. The literary success was accompanied by a move to the small screen, with a Channel 4 series called *Nigella Bites*. And a few years after launching her cookery career, in 2002, she launched her own cookware range, Living Kitchen, which is valued at £7 million. Mary has great respect for Nigella too. She told *Stella* magazine: 'She's so glamorous, with so much presence... wonderfully clever. I was in awe of her. No wonder people follow her – she's a powerhouse.'

Another example of a cook developing into a brand is Delia Smith, who has sold 14 million books and whose television programmes attract millions of viewers. She published her first recipe in 1969. If ever there was evidence needed to prove Delia's personal marketing clout, her name even made it into the dictionary. Much has been written over the years about this so-called 'Delia Effect', in particular after the publication of her hugely successful *How To Cook* books, the first of which was released in 1998, and tied in with her TV series of the same name. The 'Delia Effect' was used to describe the phenomenon whereby supermarket shelves were suddenly emptied of particular items after they had featured on her shows. There was reportedly a 10 per cent rise in egg sales in Britain as a result of the series, for example. A struggling Lancashire firm was brought back from the brink of collapse after Delia used their omelette pan on her show and described it as a 'little gem'. Sales went through the roof and the firm reported that they went from selling 200 pans a year to 90,000 in four months. Other ingredients that instantly went out of stock included cranberries – there was apparently a national shortage in 1995 – as well as vegetable bouillon powder, limes and kitchen kit such as pestles and mortars. Sea salt, prunes and instant mashed potato were also boosted by Delia's recommendations. The phenomenon suggested that celebrity cooks could have a powerful influence on our eating habits, and this was not just restricted to Delia Smith.

By 2001, after the third and final *How To Cook* book was published, the 'Delia Effect' was such a frequently used phrase that it was entered into the Collins English Dictionary. The BBC reported that the noun 'Delia' was included in a new edition of the dictionary after publishers had found that it had passed into everyday usage. Using a computer database of 418 million words that were spoken and written in English, pooled from various television shows, books, conversations and newspapers, a staggering 700 references to 'Delia' were found. Other entries in the dictionary centred around Delia's name included a 'Delia dish', described as a recipe or the 'style of cooking of British cookery writer Delia Smith', as well as 'Delia power' and 'Doing a Delia'. Speaking about her inclusion in the dictionary, Delia said at the time to Radio 4's *Today* programme: 'I think it's quite extraordinary. I've been doing recipes for about 30 years now and I suppose it's because I've been around a long time. My husband had the best remark – he said it's not bad for somebody who can't spell.'

Jeremy Butterworth, from Collins Dictionaries, said at the time: 'Delia has become part of the language in a very special way.'

Mary herself admits that Delia is one of a kind and has frequently referred to the fact that she is impressed with everything she has achieved. 'I think Delia is marvellous,' Mary told the *Daily Mail*. 'Though I have the advantage of having children who say, "Mummy, you look dreadful, get your hair sorted out," or whatever. Delia is on a pedestal, uncriticised, whereas I get the home truths.'

Christmas food sales have been transformed by the triumvirate of Jamie, Nigella and Delia. Both Jamie and Nigella recommend goose fat to help cook roast potatoes and get them crispy, and supermarkets have all said sales of the product have experienced unprecedented growth around that time of year as a result. The *Daily Telegraph* reported that, at Sainsbury's, sales of cinnamon sticks in 2009 were up 200 per cent on the same time the previous year, while sales of Marsala wine, an ingredient in Delia's panettone trifle, increased by 300 per cent. Sales of pickled walnuts doubled after Delia coupled them with braised venison in a recipe. The newspaper reported that her recipe for chestnut cupcakes also caused shoppers to stock up on new ingredients, including *crème de marrons*, a sweetened chestnut purée, and chestnut flour, which hadn't been stocked by the retailer until Delia's series *Classic Christmas*. A spokesman told the newspaper: 'Every year we get calls about the ingredients that feature in celebrity chef tips. In the past we have answered calls on goose fat, cranberries and, last year, semolina due to Nigella Lawson's roast potato tip, with sales shooting through the roof. This year calls have led to us stocking the unusual chestnut flour in our special selection range,' said a spokesman for the stores. And, of course, Mary would always have her own part to play in helping thousands of people around Christmas time. Her trusted Christmas recipes, books and writings in *Good Food* magazine would be relied upon during the festive season.

A 2009 BBC programme, *The Rise of the Superchef*, discussed how celebrity chefs have changed the British attitude to food forever. One woman, Borra Garson, even set up a talent agency just to manage celebrity chefs, with Jamie Oliver one of her first clients. She oversaw the signing of his contract with Sainsbury's, worth a reported £1 million.

'When they first approached, I can't say that he was 100 per cent convinced this would be a good move,' she recalled. 'We talked endlessly about it before he decided to sign on the dotted line. I remember leaving the law firm, after Jamie signed the contract, and I turned to him in the elevator and I said: "Congratulations, you're now officially a millionaire."'

Merchandising also brings in the money for today's celebrity chef. Fiona Lindsay, who runs Limelight Celebrity Management, the agency which helps Mary promote herself and her products, says the popularity of goods with a name behind them lies in that person's reliability. 'We're buying trust,' she has said. 'We're buying into reliability, but we're also buying a part of the celebrity; a piece of our favourite celebrity chef.' That reliability is what people love about Mary. In a 2010 poll to find the most trusted cookery writer, she was in the top three alongside Jamie Oliver and Delia Smith. Her fans just know that her recipes will work.

Daughter Annabel says the success of her mother's brand taught her the most important lesson of her life. 'Mum worked from the bottom up, and she instilled in me a work ethic which is there to this day,' Annabel told *Yours* magazine. 'As young as five I remember accompanying her to demonstrations and helping with little jobs like grating cheese!' The business has gone from strength to strength. Meanwhile, outside of work Annabel has continued to have a zest for life – with her mother describing her as the 'artistic' one of her three children. Among her hobbies are travelling, snowboarding, fishing, sailing, scuba diving, swimming and camping in a tepee, with which she has travelled the world. As the business ticked over, Annabel flew to Australia, where she worked on a fishing trawler for a brief stint, then took a diving course in the Galápagos islands, trekked in the Amazon rainforest and worked in a restaurant in Goa in western India. Among all that, she also met Dan Bosger, an experienced businessman himself, while she was travelling in Kenya. They married in 2002 before going on to give Mary three more grandchildren – Louis, Hobie and Atalanta. The grandchildren are a constant source of delight for Mary and Paul – and a frequent source of laughter. 'The grandchildren being naughty when they think that none of the grown-ups can see them,' was once Mary's reply to a question about what made her laugh.

Annabel's rich life experience only added to her relationship with Mary, whom she came to see as not only her mother, but also her best friend and business partner. 'We work well together because we both like to experiment,' said Annabel in the interview with *Yours* magazine. 'We meet halfway and are not afraid to criticise each other. Mum has always been, and continues to be, a huge inspiration to me. She inspired me to try different flavours, to see what went together, to extend my palate. And I can't believe she works more now than ever before! But it's her fuel; it's what she was born to do.'

Meanwhile, Mary remains proud of her daughter and is impressed by her worldly-wise ways. 'She's well travelled, far more than me, so she brings lots of different foods and flavours from around the world. And she does love cooking. Isn't that lucky for a young wife and mother? You're going to be doing it for your whole life, so you might as well enjoy it!'

Twenty-one years later, the business is still going strong, with Annabel also managing to balance her home life with the family business. In fact, even more of the family became involved in it. Paul became the business's company secretary – and Annabel describes him both as a 'very brave man' and the 'backbone of the company' for taking up the role. While also running his own business, Tom took shares out in the family business. Meanwhile, Sir Robin Buchanan, chairman of Michael Page International plc, the global specialist recruitment company, became a close family friend of the Berrys. He often helps out with the direction of the business and became what Annabel described as 'our family mentor', often dispensing business advice and helping to give them all an outside perspective.

While Mary remains the face of the sauces, Annabel continues to run the business day to day, organising photo shoots, liaising with press officers, dealing with overseas customers, ordering stock and arranging new products and food shows to plug their brand. But while Annabel works tirelessly to continue to expand the business, she admits it wouldn't have happened without her parents. 'Mum and I get along very well,' says Annabel. 'We work together on new ideas, marketing and product development. We share an office and she is pretty good at leaving me to get on with my business! Mary Berry & Daughter Dressings and Sauces has always been my baby but I could never have done it without Mum and Dad.' Annabel admits she often needs to take holidays to help detach from the business, because at times it can become all-consuming. 'If we're out together then we will always discuss "the empire" as we call it,' Annabel says. 'But that is a pleasure to us because we are all so shocked by its success. It's a real family affair – if we're testing something new we'll all sit round the dinner table, and my father and brother can be very blunt! But the family is the backbone of the whole thing.'

The success of the range is doubtless testament to the bond Mary shares with her family. Their love for one another inevitably helped spur the business on and brought them even closer. But the business aside, it's plain to see from all the interviews Mary has conducted over the years that family is the most important thing to her. In particular, she dotes on her grandchildren, with whom she loves cooking. 'We do all sorts – cupcakes, omelettes, fruit skewers, lasagne… We cook the things they like; that's the secret to getting them involved. And it's very educational, all the weighing of ingredients and working out timings. It's a great thing to do with children.'

So while business and family have often come together to bring success for Mary, it's still important for her to spend quality time with them, away from the 'empire'. Such occasions include Christmas, which is big in the Berry household. It combines the two ingredients in life that Mary most values – home cooking and her family.

'Food is the one thing that doesn't worry me at Christmas because I know all about it,' said Mary in the *Daily Telegraph*. 'Throughout the year, I work on new and inventive cooking, but at this time of year, I keep things traditional. Breakfast is no feast in our house at Christmas. There are just croissants, toast and marmalade, fresh fruit and real orange juice. For lunch, I am in charge, but there are always lots of helpers. It is the one day of the year when we use the dining room and I decorate the table with red amaryllis in vases tied with red ribbon. We always have a turkey because it goes an awfully long way. I do chestnut stuffing with apricots separately, so it goes crispy, plus red cabbage, sprouts or leeks, puréed celeriac, cocktail sausages – the grandchildren love those – and masses of sauces. Afterwards, we have home-made Christmas pudding with brandy butter and then Christmas cake and tea when we get back from our walk.'

But even if her grandchildren don't follow in her footsteps in the kitchen, it's obvious that simply being surrounded by them is good enough for Mary. In an interview with *The Lady*, Mary was asked when she was at her happiest. She replied: 'I'm very happy at home – my young are around me … We're a good team and I wouldn't have them if I were anywhere else. Fantasy is reality; I'm very lucky.' Like many of us, Mary says she wouldn't hesitate to 'gather up every one of my family photographs' if she had to save anything from a house fire. Looking back on her life, Mary admits she would never want to recapture her youth. Happiness, it seems, has come with age. 'I don't miss anything about my youth,' Mary told the

Daily Mail. 'It's good to be 76, because you get so well looked after. It's always been "Mum will do it" for my children. Now they're so thoughtful. I've run around after them and it's payback time! It's not the thought of dying that scares me, but living without my husband. I'd like us both to die in our sleep together. Real old age, as I've seen with my mother, can be hard and lonely. You don't want to be a burden on your children. Even when she was 104, my mother came for Christmas and said, "You must leave things for me to do. Let me do the sprouts." I just pray I don't linger too long.'

But despite her present contentment, there was a moment in Mary's life that would call into question whether she would ever be able to find that happiness. It involved her youngest child, William.

CHAPTER 5

SAVED
BY CAKE

It was a night Mary Berry will never forget; etched on her mind for evermore. It wasn't the first night of a new show of hers on TV. Nor was it the launch of her latest cookery book. In fact, it was the simple act of cooking a lamb roast dinner one Friday evening in June 1989. It was something Mary did so regularly that, at the time, it didn't seem out of the ordinary. But it would become what she has since described as one of the most important meals she's ever cooked.

Mary's youngest child William, then 19, had recently returned home from Bristol Polytechnic. He had completed his first year at the institution where he had enrolled the previous autumn as a business studies student. It's fair to say he was doing brilliantly – his work was going well and he had made lots of friends. As with all their children, Mary and Paul had wanted to give William the best possible start in life. Prior to Bristol he had studied at

Gordonstoun School, the private boarding school in Moray, Scotland.

Gordonstoun was founded in 1933 by Dr Kurt Hahn, formerly headmaster of Salem School in southern Germany. Dr Hahn fled Germany in 1933 under threat from the Nazis for standing firm in the face of aggression. Perceiving decay in the society of the day, he aimed to foster in young people skill, compassion, honesty, initiative, adventure and a sense of service towards their fellow human beings. Hahn was fortunate to find an attractive, imposing estate in the temperate environment of Morayshire. With a handful of boys, the school began with two historic seventeenth-century buildings, Gordonstoun House and Round Square, built by the famed eccentric, Sir Robert Gordon, the so-called Wizard of Gordonstoun. The school grew from there. During the 1960s Prince Charles attended the school on the recommendation of his father, the Duke of Edinburgh, who had been one of its first pupils. Although Princess Anne didn't attend, she sent her two children, Zara and Peter Phillips. Other notable alumni include Balthazar Getty, Hollywood actor and heir to the Getty oil fortune, writer William Boyd, saxophonist Dick Heckstall-Smith, cricketer Preston Mommsen and Olympic rower Heather Stanning, who won Olympic gold at London 2012 in the women's pairs.

The school instilled in William a sense of hard work and loyalty through its ethos of the Four Pillars of Education, with each pillar representing a part of the whole curriculum—internationalism, challenge, responsibility and service. There was one blot on William's copy book, though: a prank played when he was 16, which led to Gordonstoun 'sending him down' (meaning the school authorities suspended him temporarily) for half a term to give him time to reflect on what he had done. But William returning home meant that Mary was able to get even closer to her son – something she would soon come to cherish for the rest of her life. 'I had a very happy time with him, not ticking him off, and I learnt a lot about him,' Mary told the *Mail on Sunday*. In interviews years later, Mary would describe William as her 'bright button'.

Now, having finishing his first stint at Bristol, he was back home in Buckinghamshire. And like the doting mother she is, Mary wanted to spoil him. As was often the case in the Berry household, Mary wanted all of her family to enjoy dinner together. Rarely a day would go by without the family gathering around the kitchen table for an evening meal, where they would catch up on what they had all been up to. But as that night was a special occasion, Mary had laid out the dining-room table with the best crockery and china.

Perhaps like a typical teenager, William wasn't sure what all the fuss was about. He walked into the dining room just as his mum was putting the final touches to the table and looked confused. 'William walked in and he said, "Who's coming?"' Mary recalled in an interview with the *Mail on Sunday*. '"You!" I told him. "It's for you. And it's your favourite."' She added, in her interview with *Desert Island Discs*: 'I remember the night before we had supper in the dining room and we had roast lamb, and I had really gone to a lot of trouble because it was lovely to have him home.'

The meal itself went off without a hitch, as meals in that

household always did, with Paul and the kids doubtless enjoying second helpings.

But the next morning, everything would change. Nothing was out of the ordinary to begin with. William woke up as usual. It was sunny for that time of year and he decided he wanted to go out to buy a copy of *The Times*. So interested was he in his business studies, he regularly kept on top of the day's financial news – even on a Saturday. William asked to borrow a car to nip to the village. The only one available was his father's sports car, which had recently been restored. Paul had spent such time, effort and money on the refurbishment that Mary was unsure. So she called Paul, who by this point was at work at his antiques shop, to ask whether he was OK with William using the car.

'We had had a sports car restored, and I said, well just ask Dad,' she said during her appearance on *Desert Island Discs*. 'And it was a January morning with the sun streaming in the windows, and so Paul said absolutely fine, off you go.' Annabel decided she would go with William and they grabbed the keys to the car and rushed off.

Mary went about her business as usual, working around the house and starting to prepare lunch as she usually would late on a Saturday morning. But after a while William and Annabel hadn't returned. 'When the two of them didn't come back for lunch I thought: "That's funny,"' Mary told the *Daily Mail*. But she simply assumed they had got sidetracked and were taking a little longer than usual.

But the tragic reality of the situation was about to unfold. As she sat waiting for her children, she became increasingly worried. She perched herself on a window seat overlooking her home's pretty courtyard and, as she looked out, one of the most ominous things she has ever seen appeared. A policeman walked up the drive to the family home. Instantly Mary knew it was bad news. 'When the policeman came to the door I knew why,' Mary told the *Mail on Sunday*. 'I was more sorry for him than I was for me. It was so difficult for him to tell me.'

The news was just as bad as Mary feared – William had been killed and Annabel was in hospital. The police officer told Mary her two children had been involved in a car accident. William, who had been at the wheel, had driven too fast around a corner and the car had collided with another vehicle before flipping over. William had died almost instantly on impact, while Annabel had been rescued from the wreckage of the car.

And as the policeman imparted the news, Mary's world collapsed. 'You know, the moment the policeman comes to the door you know exactly,' she told *Desert Island Discs*. 'And he said that sadly William had died, and Annabel was in hospital.' The officer didn't know how badly injured Annabel was and so Mary's immediate reaction was to assume that Annabel would also die. She said it was a 'ghastly' moment, in an interview with the *Daily Mail*. 'I thought: "Oh no, not two".' Understandably, Mary's head was spinning. She couldn't understand how the accident had happened. 'He was normally such a careful driver but that day he simply drove too fast,' Mary later told the paper.

Struggling to contain her emotions, Mary immediately called Paul and told him the devastating news. He immediately rushed home from work. Then at 3pm the police officer took Mary and Paul to Wycombe Hospital where Annabel was being treated. As they sat in the waiting room, Mary was trying to come to terms with everything – her youngest son had died and the fate of her only daughter was unknown. Moments later, there was at least one bit of welcome news.

'I can remember them giving us sweet tea and saying sit down and being really nice,' Mary told *Desert Island Discs*. 'Then I saw a pink tracksuit covered in mud running up the corridor,' said Mary to the *Daily Mail*. It was Annabel; she had managed to escape with minor cuts and bruises. 'I thought: "At least we have Annabel,"' Mary told the *Daily Mail*.

Then the nurses at the hospital approached the Berrys. They wondered if they wanted to see William's body. Despite it being one of the most gut-wrenching moments of her life, Mary was adamant that it was something that she wanted to do. 'People say: "Should you go and see them?" but there was never any hesitation in my mind,' Mary said. 'That's a good thing to do. I wanted to know.' Irrespective of her initial determination to go through with it, as Mary approached the hospital ward she realised how difficult it was going to be. 'The nurses said, "Do you want to see William?" And I said, "Oh, yes!" And then I thought: "What have I said?"' she said in an interview with the *Mail on Sunday*. 'Is he going to be damaged? But he wasn't. They had laid him in a bed and I don't know what they did but he was so beautiful and I could touch him ... He was so cold but you'd never know he was. He was perfect. You could just see the front of his face and it wasn't even bruised. He was just my Will.'

As she was struggling to come to terms with it all, funeral

directors arrived at the hospital. Amidst all the emotion, it gave Mary a focus that helped her deal with the reality of her son's death. She was insistent that his funeral service should be a quiet, low-key affair for close family and friends to pay their respects to the William they loved. 'Later, when the funeral director came, all sober, asking how many beautiful brass handles we wanted on the coffin, I said, "Let's have the most simple. It's just a little chap going to heaven. We don't need all this pomp."'

For weeks, Mary couldn't bring herself to do anything. Life came to a standstill and she had to take time off work. 'The shock rendered me incapable of functioning,' Mary wrote in the *Daily Mail*. 'I couldn't do a thing ... I certainly didn't eat, even though people were rallying round and bringing me meals. I remember eating soup, but very little else.'

For the rest of her life Mary will, understandably, always be affected by William's death. Even more than 20 years later, having been asked about it endlessly, there's rarely an interview where Mary doesn't become understandably emotional as she relives those harrowing moments and comes to terms all over again with what happened. But, bravely, she has always remained philosophical, despite the tragedy. 'There is a prominent memorial in the local church, erected by unknown parents who lost all three of their sons,' she told the *Mail on Sunday*. 'I told myself to get a grip: "I've only lost one. Come on!"' She reminds herself how lucky she is even today. 'I have everything else but William.'

It's a stoicism that few could muster, but all would admire. It was doubtless something she was able to achieve thanks to the support and love from her family. In the weeks, months and years following William's death, Mary admits that they became even closer than before.

'Since the accident, we've become very close as a family. His death has taught me all sorts of things,' she told the *Daily Mail*. Not least she values the importance of having the family all around the table for a meal more than she ever did before. She knows that every meal might be the last that you have with all the people you love together. 'We were all as a complete family the night before [William died],' she told *Desert Island Discs*, 'which is a huge bonus because I remember that.'

'William was the cleverest of my children,' Mary told the *Daily Mail*. 'I feel sorry for people who have a row and then something like that happens. William went out on a high. We'd had a lovely supper the night before. A child's death can split up a family but it brought us closer. My children became really protective of each other. Paul and I were emotionally drained but we were a pair. I hadn't the heart to go to work because I didn't want to leave Paul alone. We lived on soup. I used to be 11 stone but I went down to eight, just pining for William. Our good friends were amazingly supportive. Will's death made me quite a different person. Little things don't bother me now. If nobody's hurt, I'm like an old boot. The other week, I backed my car into a wall and I didn't even get out to look. When my mother died recently, at the age of 105, I was quite matter-of-fact about it. I just thought, thank goodness for her. I'm ashamed about it but I'm not grieving at all.'

Aside from treating every meal like it may be her last and valuing family more than ever before, William's death taught Mary a number of other life lessons. Surprisingly, neighbours in Mary's home village would studiously avoid her in the aftermath of William's death. Maybe it was merely a case of them going about things with a typically English stiff upper lip. Whatever was the case, Mary has responded to this by doing quite the opposite if the tables are ever turned. 'If there's a tragedy in someone else's family I would automatically go straight up to them and talk to them. Because when it happened to us, even some people we knew would cross the road to avoid talking to us. But the best thing you can do is go up to them and let them talk. The worst thing you can say is: "You'll get over it." You feel like socking them when they say that. You never get over it; you learn to live with it,' Mary told the *Daily Mail*.

Over the years, Mary has had a number of ways of keeping William's memory alive. When he was little, he planted a Christmas tree in the back garden of their house. It remains there to this day and Mary says that every time she walks past it she thinks of him. Framed photographs of William are on every surface in her house and her five grandchildren all know who he is … their Uncle William, whom they never met but will always know. Perhaps even more poignantly, Mary says she has had to learn to say she has two children rather than three whenever she is asked – something that any parent can understand is particularly hard.

The incredible strength that Mary showed in the way she handled William's death is something that she demonstrates time and time again. 'We were lucky to have him. And if he walked through the door now I would say, "Where have you been, young man? Come on,"' she told the *Daily Mail*. 'It doesn't go. And we miss him enormously. As a family we are forever talking about Will. We remember the good and the bad; he was naughty just like the rest of the children, at times. But every family has something that happens in their lives.' While the tragedy of the situation was made even worse by William's age, in some ways Mary even admits she's glad that it happened when he was so young – rather than once he had settled down. 'I am really pleased that if he was to die, that he didn't leave a wife and children,' she said in an interview with *Mail* on *Sunday*. 'Because you know, that would have been a sadness for them. And he died at a time when he was truly successful with his sport and his school, and he was totally happy with himself. So we have really nice memories of him. He had done well.'

It's surely that fortitude that Mary shows even when dealing with the worst that life has thrown at her that has driven her on to be the successful woman – both at home and work – that she is today. However, she admitted she wouldn't have had that strength if it wasn't for baking. In the years after William died, she admits that cooking and, in particular, making cakes, acted as a sort of therapy for her. It helped her overcome the difficult moments, when she found herself missing William or feeling particularly low as a result of his death. 'I think keeping busy [helped me to cope], and my way of keeping busy was to cook,' she told Kirsty Young on *Desert Island Discs*. 'But I always look back and I think, it is a huge bonus to have two other children. I mean, if he had been the only one, shattering. And it brings you terribly close together. And Annabel and Tom, and their other halves, if we are having an occasion we will always raise a glass to Will, or we say Will would like this, or what a shame he can't see this. I think for us we like to keep him very much part of the family.' In a first-person piece she wrote for the *Daily*

Mail in 2011, she reflected on how baking had acted as a natural anti-depressant, saying: 'Getting back to cooking and baking was the only way I knew to regain some normality in my life. It isn't easy, but you get out the flour, the sugar and the eggs, and there is great comfort in the ritual. The novelist Marian Keyes certainly thinks so, having suffered from depression. She has just brought out a book called *Saved By Cake*, in which she claims that baking helped her through the darkest of times. I can completely understand Marian's point of view, as I'm sure can anyone who has been gripped by the baking bug. The idea of baking as a therapy – and an effective one at that – might seem a little far-fetched to some, but not to me. When times are tough, the way to soothe our hearts is so often through food. And food, especially cake, always tastes better when cooked with love. Anyone who thinks baking a cake is just about, well, baking a cake, probably hasn't done it that often.'

Mary says there are two clear reasons why baking is such an effective antidote to depression. 'First, it is satisfying. At a basic level, baking a cake is straightforward,' she wrote. 'You follow some basic rules (it is science, after all, albeit simple science) and, at the end of the process, you have something to show – and eat – for your efforts. How many chores, particularly around the house, can you say that about? Then there's the rich reward – carrying your beautiful Victoria sponge to the table as your children's faces light up in anticipation and they say: "Gosh, you are clever, Mum." Even after a lifetime of baking, I've never stopped getting a little buzz when that happens. Perhaps that's because when you bake, your reward is twofold. You have the pleasure of seeing a wonderful creation come out of the oven, then the pleasure of seeing what joy it brings to others. People are terribly impressed – and touched – when you bake for them. Those who don't bake see conjuring up a cake as something quite magical. It is love on a plate. But the benefits of baking aren't just for the person eating the cake or the biscuit. The actual process of baking makes you feel useful – so useful that, if you are depressed, I would go as far as to say it gives you something to get up for in the morning. I can understand how, if you are feeling low, you wallow all day then feel worse when your partner comes home and asks: "So what have you done today?" It may sound flippant, but being able to say you spent the afternoon making fairy cakes gives a sense of satisfaction and focus, even a *raison d'être*.'

But while baking helped give Mary a focus in her day-to-day routine in the wake of William's death, she also realised that she needed to get back to work eventually. It all seemed too painful to consider, though, and the prospect of returning to normality just four months after the tragedy seemed too much, too soon. At the time, Mary was still cookery editor of *Ideal Home* magazine and still a consultant for Bensons, the public relations firm where she had first got into journalism. The commute between Buckinghamshire and London understandably seemed difficult after William died. 'I needed to be at home more with my husband after the accident, but I also knew it was essential to keep busy,' Mary told *The Times*.

And so she came up with a plan to make a career change that would help her spend more time at home while continuing to work. She decided to start holding Aga Workshops in her kitchen, while continuing to write books. It seemed like the perfect solution and would signal a new stage in Mary's journey to becoming one of Britain's best-loved cooks. But in order to help with the running of the workshops she would need a personal assistant. Having an extra pair of hands would also free up Mary's time and lessen the burden of some of the smaller but time-consuming tasks such as general administration. It would allow her to get back to work, but at a slower pace than she was used to ... giving her more opportunity to deal with the grief and anguish of what had happened over the preceding few months.

A 21-year-old woman called Lucy Young heard through friends that Mary was looking for someone. Lucy had trained at a catering college and spent time working in various restaurants and for private catering firms. She was also fully aware of Mary's work, having been a dedicated reader of her cookbooks as she was growing up and while she was studying. Despite having an impressive CV for her age, Lucy assumed that she had no chance of getting the job. So when Mary decided to interview her for the post, Lucy had no expectations. 'I wasn't nervous at the interview because I didn't consider myself experienced enough to get the job,' Lucy told *The Times*. Regardless of Lucy's lack of confidence, Mary was impressed by her experience and enthusiasm. Mary also liked the fact that she talked directly and honestly. But there was something else about Lucy that struck a chord with Mary after the tragedy of losing William. Lucy was clearly someone who valued family and who realised that her siblings were precious. Mary was convinced she was the right person for the job and offered it to her immediately. 'Like me, she's a perfectionist and she spoke fondly of her brothers and parents, so I knew she'd muck in with my family. She's also passionate about food,' Mary told *The Times*.

Surprised that she had managed to bag the role despite convincing herself she wouldn't, Lucy says she was incredibly nervous to begin with. She had idolised Mary for years and couldn't believe her luck. 'I was extremely edgy for the first few months because it was too important a job to mess up,' Lucy said to *The Times*. 'As a child, I had pored over Mary's cake recipe books with my mother. She had always been one of my heroines.' Lucy started working every day at Mary's family home. But to begin with there were a few mistakes made, albeit quite minor ones. During the first week Mary went out and Lucy was left in charge with specific instructions to bake a batch of meringues. Unfortunately, three out of four of the batches went wrong and the meringues collapsed. On her return home, Mary took Lucy to one side and guided her through what she described as a 'foolproof' recipe. It was also difficult for Lucy to get used to working in Mary's home, as she had always been used to working in larger, less personal kitchens. She told *The Times*: 'It takes time to discover where people keep things and one day I couldn't find the rolling pin, so I used a milk bottle instead. To my relief, Mary praised my initiative.'

Lucy wasn't just a personal assistant to Mary. Although she perhaps didn't realise it at the time, she helped Mary through one of the most difficult times in her life. While Mary was bravely facing the world again and getting back into work, the devastating loss of William was hitting her hard. When William's friends turned up at the family home during those first few months, Lucy would invite them in for coffee if Mary wasn't around. She was an emotional support to her boss – and it was something Mary would never forget. Lucy became part of the family and, as such, Mary trusted her, and saw her as a confidante and someone she could rely on day in, day out. Mary's other two children, Annabel and Tom, became close to Lucy too, and they would all often lunch together with Paul – although he insisted that they weren't allowed to talk about cooking on those occasions. 'I was flattered to be drawn into such a warm family,' Lucy told *The Times*.

Gradually Lucy became more and more involved in Mary's work, and was soon an integral part of her boss's career. She would track down lost recipes for people who wrote to Mary, and deal with the hundreds upon hundreds of requests for Mary to attend events and functions as her celebrity status started to grow. And while at first Lucy may have been hesitant about her role and abilities, she soon gained confidence, learning what to say yes to and what to say no to on Mary's behalf. 'I feel protective towards her. She'd do too much if I didn't stop her,' Lucy told *The Times*.

Soon Lucy's role wasn't restricted to working at Mary's house. She began travelling around the country with her and was always at her side for the 30 or more demonstrations she gave every year. They also devised recipes together for Mary's Aga Workshops. 'We'll sit at the kitchen table with a pad and paper and say, "We need two more chicken recipes,"' Lucy told *The Times*. 'Or, "Supposing we do something with asparagus?" Neither of us gets offended if the other says "Horrid!" We work on until we're both satisfied with the result.' Of course no one could ever replace William, but the growing bond between Mary and Lucy fast became, in some ways, more akin to that between mother and daughter, rather than strictly boss and employee. Mary could see fantastic qualities in Lucy and wanted to nurture her. When it came to recipes, she realised that Lucy had great intuition. So much so that she decided Lucy should start to help her write her cookery books. To begin with, Lucy would help out with ideas for the books, but then gradually they started to co-author them, including the best-selling entertaining bible *Cook Up A Feast*. Meanwhile, as Mary's TV appearances became more frequent Lucy was always watching in the wings, making sure her boss didn't mix up the ingredients or put a foot wrong. 'It's easy to do when you are under pressure, so it's reassuring to know that someone is checking,' Mary told *The Times*. Later, Mary encouraged Lucy to start writing her own books, and soon publishers were snapping them up. Lucy's works include *The Secrets of Aga Cakes*, *The Secrets of Aga Puddings* and *Secrets from a Country Kitchen*, which have all flown off the shelves and become best-sellers. Mary confesses that she loves to make Lucy's recipes when she has the chance – surely the highest compliment any aspiring chef could be paid. 'She never tests out her recipes in my kitchen, so it was lovely getting the book and having a look at all her creations. It's a book packed with young, fun ideas and I like it very much,' Mary said in an interview with the *Independent*, on the subject of one of Lucy's books. Lucy herself also spoke passionately about her own Aga – which she came to love perhaps as much as her boss – to the Aga Living blog. She said: 'I love my new Aga. I first saw a pale blue Aga about 25 years ago and fell in love with it then, before I even had an Aga. My last one was cream, which went perfectly with the kitchen in my old house. But when Aga launched the Duck Egg Blue model for its foundry's 300th anniversary, I absolutely knew the next time I bought an Aga it would be in that colour. I'm thrilled with it and it's amazing how many people on Facebook have said that the picture I posted of it convinced them that they should choose the same colour. I'm so in love with it I've even painted my front door in the same colour. When you stand at the front of the house and open the door you look down and can see the Aga. I started cooking on it before the kitchen was even finished. The first thing I cooked was fillet steaks in a brandy sauce. It was Christmas Eve and the kitchen was a building site. I stood among piles of rubble, with the plaster drying on the walls, with just the Aga and a trestle table in the kitchen. We didn't even have a sink – just a bowl of water. I couldn't wait to cook on it!'

And after years of working for Mary, Lucy has become a well-known media figure in her own right. As well as researching and writing her books, she regularly broadcasts and contributes pieces in the press on all aspects of food and cookery. She was a regular guest on the *Great Food Live* and *Great Food Bites* – the live food shows broadcast on the satellite channel UKTV Food. She's also been interviewed a number of times on BBC Radio 2 and regularly on local radio. She's become a member of The Guild of Food Writers, the UK's respected professional association of food writers and broadcasters. Established in 1984, it now has over 400 authors, broadcasters, columnists and journalists among its members. It aims to broaden the range of members' knowledge and experience by bringing them together at

Guild events and via interviews, as well as trying to get the public more interested in food writing in general.

Lucy has written regular monthly recipes for *Country Kitchen Magazine* and a column for regular magazine *Aga Living,* which was packed full of tips and advice for making the most out of a cast-iron range. Lucy has also written individual articles for many magazines including *Antony Worrall Thompson at Home, BBC Homes and Antiques* magazine and *Rachel Allen at Home.* Lucy's media work has become so high profile and her expertise so valued that she even has an agent to field requests for her time.

As a result of her incredible talents it's unsurprising that Lucy has received countless other job offers in the world of catering. She has adamantly refused all of them. Mary, the woman she looked up to as a child, is the only person she wants to work for. 'This is my perfect job,' she told *The Times.* 'I wouldn't want to do anything else. No one else could match up to her.' And her loyalty is something Mary cherishes. When Mary started advertising for an assistant in those dark months after William's death, she could never have imagined that she would still be working with that same person more than two decades later. But as Mary regularly says, she feels she couldn't live without Lucy. Not surprisingly, Mary seems to associate Lucy with helping her get her life back on track after the devastation of William's death, and their friendship is bound to endure. 'I had no idea back then we would still be working together,' Mary told the *Daily Express.* 'There has never been a cross word between us and I value her opinion on everything. Although Lucy is a lot younger than me, we have a wonderful friendship and she gets on fantastically with my family.'

Something else that helps put what happened with William into context is the charity work that Mary has done since. After Mary spoke openly about the struggle she and her family had to come to terms with what happened to William, she was approached by one organization – Child Bereavement UK – that had been touched by her story. It was founded on 24 September 1994 by Jenni Thomas OBE, who worked with the charity for its first 15 years. Jenni began her career in the NHS, working in the special care baby unit (SCBU) at Amersham Hospital, and then in maternity and paediatric units, first at the Royal Berkshire Hospital in Reading and then at Wycombe General Hospital SCBU, in High Wycombe. It was while working in these specialist units that Jenni realised that the emotional needs of bereaved families were not being fully met, and that the staff caring for these families had been given little training in how to support them. Jenni has said: 'I realised we were very good at providing nursing and medical care when a baby was very ill but were less able to communicate and engage with parents when their baby was not expected to live or had died.' Jenni trained as a counsellor and later studied humanistic psychology and person-centred art therapy. In 1985, she set up the first bereavement counsellor post in the NHS at Wycombe General Hospital. Having identified the need for a new approach to bereavement, she put protocols and policies in place across all areas of patient care. From accident and emergency units to chaplaincy departments, Jenni educated and encouraged staff to act as advocates for vulnerable, grieving families – and it was to these families that Jenni turned to guide her work and provide input into the many training resources that she designed and produced. She then did a stint at the Oxford Regional Health Authority, where she worked as a maternity and paediatric bereavement facilitator, during which time she wrote her first book, *Supporting Parents when their Baby Dies*, aimed at professionals, and the training videos *Death at Birth* and *When Our Baby Died*. When Jenni first started the charity it was called the Child Bereavement Trust, before being renamed the Child Bereavement Charity and later Child Bereavement UK. For several years the charity was based in Jenni's home, and for many years her mother, Joan Brown, was an invaluable support and donated her own home for storage of the charity's resources. Dr Geoffrey Guy gave his premises in Harley Street, London, for training courses. The work of the charity was launched and established with Julia Samuel as founder–patron at the Royal College of Nursing, with Diana, Princess of Wales, attending the opening ceremony.

Child Bereavement UK supports families through the trauma of losing a loved one – and educates professionals in how to help the bereaved. Practically, the charity says they hope to ensure the accessibility of high-quality child bereavement support and information to all families. But it's not just families they want to help. They hope to help train professionals, by improving training across the country and maintaining the high standards needed to care for struggling families. Mary was familiar with the charity before they approached her. The organisation is based in Saunderton, Buckinghamshire, near Mary's family home, and she became aware of the charity partly because of their annual Snowdrop Walk, which is held to raise funds for families every year in

Top: A photo from the mid 1970s of Mary cooking with children Annabel, Thomas and William.

© *Rex Features*

Bottom: British home economist and broadcaster Marguerite Patten in 1960 *(left)*. She popularised simple yet healthy eating, such as at this cookery show at the London Palladium *(right)* with husband-and-wife entertainers Teddy Johnson and Pearl Carr.

© *Press Association Images*

Top left: Mary puts the finishing touch to a dish on *Afternoon Plus*.

Mary's cookery books have been trusted by millions of people for decades. Here she is pictured *(above)* at a signing of *Real Fast Food* in 2005, and *(left)* promoting the bestselling *Mary Berry's Complete Cookbook* in 2012.

© *Rex Features*

Mary, pictured bottom left with Lorraine Pascale, blazed the trail for TV chefs as we know them today: *(clockwise from top left)* Delia Smith, Jamie Oliver, Gordon Ramsay, Nigella Lawson and Rachel Khoo.

Top: Mary and her trusted PA Lucy Young.

Bottom: Charity work is very important to Mary, who supports causes close to her heart. She is pictured here at a charity clay pigeon shoot. © *Rex Features*

Mary guides Alan Titchmarsh to culinary success – and even occasionally allows him to lend a hand – on his daytime TV show. Edd Kimber, who won the first series of *Great British Bake Off*, puts in an appearance in 2011 (*bottom right*).

A huge hit with viewers, *Great British Bake Off* has also garnered nominations and awards from within the industry.

Top: Mel Giedroyc, Sue Perkins, Mary and Paul Hollywood arriving at the Arquiva British Academy Television Awards. *© Press Association Images*

Bottom left: Mary and Paul pose for the press at the Royal Television Society's RTS Programme Awards. *© Press Association Images*

Bottom right: Mary at the BAFTA Craft Awards in May 2012. *© Rex Features*

Top: Mary and Paul discuss the final of *Great British Bake Off* series three on *Loose Women*.

Bottom: Mary is a regular guest on TV chat shows such as *Daybreak* and *Lorraine Live (inset)* to encourage the country to get baking and cooking simple, healthy dishes.

© *Rex Features*

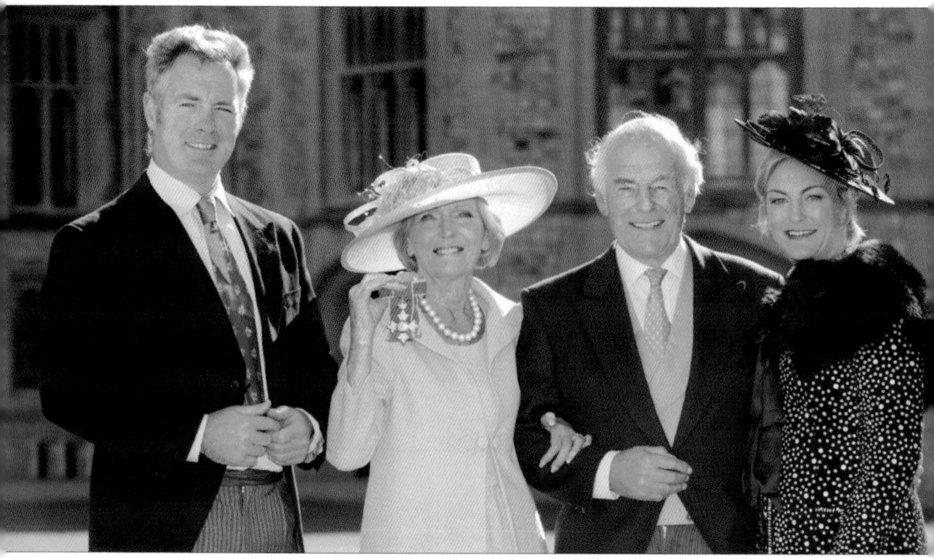

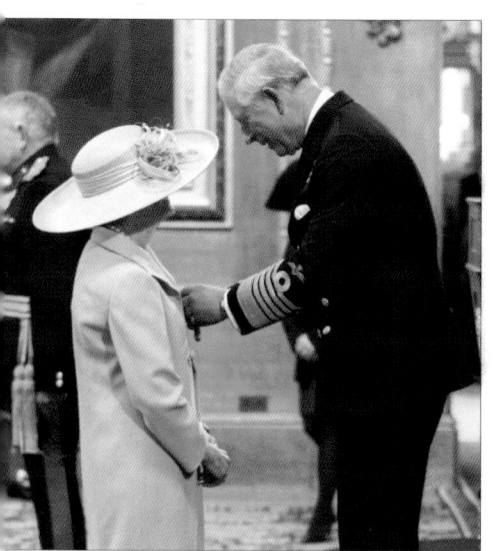

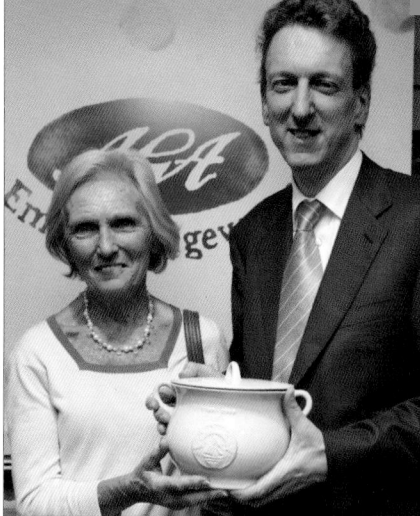

Top: Mary with (from left to right) son Tom, husband Paul and daughter Annabel, after she became a CBE at Windsor Castle.

Bottom left: HRH The Prince of Wales makes Mary a Commander of the British Empire at an investiture in October 2012.

Bottom right: But it's not the first time she's been recognised for her work – here she is presented with a commemorative pot by Aga Chief Executive William McGrath as they toast the 300th anniversary of Aga.

© Press Association Images

West Wycombe Park, and is a big event in the county's calendar. Mary was certainly aware of the lack of access to good-quality support when William died, with there being little or no support other than from her immediate friends and family. Child Bereavement UK say they believe all families should have the support they need to rebuild their lives when a child dies.

Today the charity delivers training across a breadth of issues to around 5,000 professionals at the front line of bereavement support. The charity – which relies mostly on public donations – counts Prince William, the broadcasters Sir Michael Parkinson and Alan Titchmarsh, chef Antony Worrall Thompson and theatre, TV and film actor Daniel Casey among its patrons. The Prince's mother, Diana, Princess of Wales, backed the charity during her lifetime. Prince William understood the value of the charity and the good work it did. He pledged his own support, saying: 'What my mother recognised then – and what I understand now – is that losing a close family member is one of the hardest experiences that anyone can ever endure.' Mary was herself asked to join Prince William, Sir Michael Parkinson and others to become a patron of the charity in 2009. Recognising the good work the charity does to help families that are in exactly the same situation as she had so sadly been in, Mary enthusiastically accepted. As part of her work with the charity she has met and worked with families being helped by the charity through hard times, just as she had gone through. It has been, Mary says, a heartwarming experience to know there is support out there for families going through what she did back in 1989. She has also been a vocal supporter of her local newspaper the *Bucks Free*

Press's Christmas Appeals, which aimed to raise vital funds for the charity. She told the paper: 'When my son died, people would cross the road to avoid me ... The charity helps you meet others in the same boat.' Speaking more generally about her work with the charity, Mary said: 'When William died, there was little support available for bereaved families. Through my links with Child Bereavement UK, I have met families who have received and benefited from their services. I think it's a wonderful charity and I am delighted to be a patron.'

Child Bereavement UK wasn't the only charity that Mary got involved with, as she later lent her support to the National Osteoporosis Society, becoming a patron of that organisation as well. Osteoporosis is a disease of the bones that leads to an increased risk of fracture. It literally means 'porous bones' and is often referred to as 'fragile bone disease'. Broken wrists, hips and spinal bones are the most common fractures in people with osteoporosis and it is most widespread in the elderly, although younger people can sometimes be affected. This crippling disease affects tens of thousands of people in the UK, with the charity estimating that one in two women and one in five men over the age of 50 in the UK will fracture a bone, mainly due to poor bone health. The charity was established in 1986 when doctors at a Bath hospital realised that people were worryingly unaware of osteoporosis. Back in 1986 few people had even heard of osteoporosis, and there were no national campaigns to raise awareness of the disease and the steps that can be taken to prevent it. Life for those affected by osteoporosis back then was tough, especially in terms of diagnosis. Patients were only identified as having osteoporosis if they were fortunate enough to have a doctor with a specific interest in the disease. The charity has since grown into a well-respected national concern with approximately 25,000 members and over 50 members of staff. The charity runs public health campaigns, support groups and events as well as a helpline manned by nurses with specialist knowledge of osteoporosis and bone health. Landmarks in the charity's history include receiving support from the Queen in 1990, and launching the first National Osteoporosis Week in 1994. The charity's public profile was raised further in 2001 with the appointment of Camilla, Duchess of Cornwall, as president, and in 2005 the government announced £20 million extra funding for DXA bone density scanners in England after tireless campaigning by the organisation.

The charity's core aims resonated with Mary, who has always passionately believed in the value of good cooking in helping to achieve and maintain good health. And as someone in her seventies, Mary also understood that it was a disease that particularly affects the older generations. Not only has Mary supported the charity generally, meeting workers from the organisation and seeing first-hand the work they do, but she has also put her culinary expertise to good use in order to raise funds. She helped run the charity's Bone Appétit campaign – a drive by the organisation to get people around the country to start cooking food that helps prevent bone disease and build healthier bones. Specifically, the aim of the campaign was to encourage people to host dinner parties using recipes for meals that are high in calcium, a mineral that helps maintain bone health. The aim was to get each guest to pay the equivalent of the price for a meal in a restaurant, to generate funds to support vital services, including the charity's helpline, research programme and 100-plus UK-wide support groups. Mary didn't just front the campaign, she very much led from the front – even holding one such event herself. She organised and cooked at a four-hour lunch at Ston Easton Park, near her birthplace, Bath, where she prepared a series of delicious bone-healthy recipes from her own cookbooks. Guests were treated to a two-course lunch with wine included for just £50, and all the profits went to the charity.

Another good cause wholeheartedly supported by Mary is Meningitis UK. She has opted to use the high profile her writing and presenting career has afforded her to shine a light on this charity, which funds research into preventing the devastating disease. In a letter to the *Daily Telegraph*, Mary wrote: 'As a *Great British Bake Off* judge and cookery writer, I am appealing to your readers during National Cupcake Week to get creative in the kitchen for Meningitis UK. From a Mad Hatter's tea party to a bake-off with your friends, there is so much fun you can have with the charity's Time 4 Tea fundraising initiative this autumn. Meningitis is the disease which parents fear most. To find a vaccine which would protect future generations would be a wonderful achievement. I'm offering one of my favourite cake recipes, Ginger and Treacle Spiced Traybake, to everyone who signs up.'

As far as Mary was concerned, a little charity work has been the least she can do. Despite the tragic loss of William, she feels truly blessed. Not only did she have a loving family to support her through the hard times, but she also felt she

had a calling in life in the form of baking. While William is never far from her heart, no matter what life throws at her, Mary knows she will be able to survive.

CHAPTER 6

QUEEN OF
THE AGA

Mary's love affair with the Aga started years before it would become part of her working life. She and her husband Paul first bought one of the state-of-the-art heat-storage cookers in the 1960s, when they moved from London to Buckinghamshire to settle and start a family. It was the pride and joy of Mary's kitchen, sitting right in the middle, and would come to be a huge part of her life and career in the coming years. She later said that the Aga could do 'amazing things'. And by that, she didn't just mean cooking. At first it wasn't even something she used to bake her world-famous cakes and other recipes. In fact, she used it for anything but cooking to begin with. She simply liked the ambient warmth it created at home. 'I got one just to keep warm when we moved out of London,' she told the *Daily Mail*. 'And it has other uses: I dry my cashmere on it, and I hatched a duck in the warm drawer by the side of it.' And she also told *The Times*: 'Whenever I empty the washing machine I automatically pick out things like that jumper I want to wear tonight, and carefully fold it on the simmering plate, and it is soon cosy and ready.' Those anecdotes perhaps take Mary back to her own childhood, when she was growing up in Bath and remembered bringing up little chicks at home with her parents. 'Paul found a duck egg on the village green and brought it home for breakfast,' she told the *Daily Mail*. 'But I decided to try to hatch it. It was a very ordinary mallard but William adored it. He called it Bloody Lucky.'

But of course, the Aga became an integral part of Mary's cooking life, too. It is a one-of-a-kind item. It runs on gas, oil or solid fuel. It is always turned on, and even heats all the water for the household. It comprises either two or four ovens, with half very hot and the other half warm. Two large hot plates sit on the top. The heat isn't adjustable – instead you have the equivalent of either gas mark nine or gas mark two to cook everything. The lightest of the two-oven models weighs 406kg, while the heaviest four-oven variety is a whopping 842kg, and they are currently priced between £3,775 and £10,000. When it comes to the Aga's popularity, the numbers speak for themselves. It is estimated that there are more than 800,000 in homes across the globe. The fact that the Aga was always turned on meant that Mary was always inclined to be testing out a recipe or trying to come up with something new in the oven. She says it enticed her to cook even more than usual. 'The dog and grandchildren love it, and it tempts me to cook,' said Mary in an interview with the *Daily Mail*. 'I have four ovens – for roasting, simmering, baking and warming. The roasting oven has bottom heat, so you can put things like flans in it without baking blind,' she told the paper.

The Aga company website gives a comprehensive decade-by-decade rundown of the cooker's lively and interesting history. The Aga range was invented in 1922, when the Swedish physicist Dr Gustaf Dalén came up with the idea for the world's first heat-storage cooker. He had already won the Nobel Prize for developing automatic lighthouses, which quickly became used across the globe, saving hundreds of thousands of lives and transforming the shipping and sailing industries. But Dalén had recently lost his sight after an experiment went wrong and exploded in his face. As a result he was confined to his bedroom. His wife Elma, who looked after him around the clock, was always having to fix their standard, old-fashioned cooker as it became increasingly unreliable. And, desperate for a project to keep him occupied, Dalén decided he wanted to create a cooker that was generally more efficient, to help his Elma in the kitchen. He created a cast-iron cooker capable of doing every kind of cooking simultaneously, by means of its two large hot plates and two ovens. And so the now-famous Aga was born, and by 1929 manufacturing had moved from Sweden to England, at the Aga Heat Ltd factory in Smethwick in the West Midlands. Agas became really popular during the 1930s and sales continued to grow steadily during that time. In 1931 a total of 322 Aga cookers were bought, with sales soaring to 1,705 just 12 months later. One of the keys to its success was talented salesman David Ogilvy, who went on to form the worldwide advertising giant Ogilvy Mather. He was one of the company's first salesmen and his 'The Theory and Practice of Selling an Aga Cooker' has been described by *Fortune* magazine as 'the finest instruction manual ever written'. In 1934 the *Aga Cookbook* was published by Sheila

Hibben, who explained that Dalén had 'tackled the problem with a view to creating a stove that would provide all the conveniences and economy that modern engineering demands'. The book was published in the USA, proof of the Aga cooker's growing popularity outside Britain. Years later Mary would write her own Aga cookbook, which became the bible for using the iconic stove.

In 1934, 16 members of the Graham Land Expedition Team took an Aga cooker to the Antarctic. For the next three years their Aga cooker ensured they ate well and lived in warmth and comfort, despite the temperature dropping to -40°C outside – proving that an Aga isn't just for cooking, as Mary would later discover. In the 1940s, the demand for the Aga cooker continued to grow. As the Second World War loomed, the Aga in a way helped to hold families together, as crisis gripped Europe. It started to become more than just a cooker – it was a focal point for family activities; the heart of the home. The kitchen equivalent of a roaring log fire in the living room, it was something people could congregate around even when food wasn't being prepared.

The British government placed orders for Aga cookers for canteens in munitions works, communal feeding centres and hospitals. Demand increased so dramatically that the waiting period rose to a staggering 27 weeks. A second manufacturing plant was opened in Shropshire. In 1947, the majority of manufacturing moved to the landmark Coalbrookdale foundry in Shropshire, a foundry that has been running for more than 300 years. All Aga cookers continue to be handmade here today by a team of engineers. This little village in the Ironbridge Gorge was a very fitting home for the Aga. It was here, in 1709, that Abraham Darby first smelted iron with coke, a move that kick-started the Industrial Revolution. To make an Aga, molten iron is poured into casting moulds, before every cooker is given multiple coats of vitreous enamel. The process, which takes place over a period of three days, is a world away from the process used by most modern cooker manufacturers – a quick spray-paint. Finally, every Aga component is individually inspected and colour-checked. It is such craftsmanship that helps ensure the life of an Aga cooker is measured in decades, not years. When war broke out in 1939, much of Aga Heat Ltd's production-line workers were given indefinite leave from work to help the war effort.

By the 1950s, the cooker had established itself as an essential accessory to fine living, and sales reached more than 50,000 units per year. But its history was about to become even more colourful – literally – when the Aga was rolled out in a range of different finishes. Buyers could, for the first time, have their favourite cooker in their favourite colour. For 34 years the classic Aga had been available only in cream, but in 1956 that all changed. The introduction of the new Aga De Luxe models in pale blue, pale green, grey and white proved hugely popular with Aga enthusiasts. All production had moved to Coalbrookdale by 1957, where further new models were being introduced. These included Agas that had chrome-plated domed lids. Perhaps the biggest stamp of approval came when the long-running BBC Radio 4 soap opera *The Archers* featured an Aga in Doris and Dan Archer's kitchen. Because of the difficulty of re-creating the authentic sound of an Aga door, a real Aga door had to be built in to the studio.

The 1960s saw a decline in the use of solid fuel and the

move to more convenient energy sources, such as gas and electricity. The first oil-fired cooker was introduced in 1964, followed by the launch of the first gas model in 1968. These products were the first to make use of the iconic black lozenge logo – which is still used to this day. In 1968, reflecting fashions of the time, the Aga colour palette was further extended to include dark blue, red, yellow and black. The 1970s was a decade of transition for the Aga company, as the focus shifted to innovation and the challenge of developing a new wave of Aga cookers to meet the demands of the next generation of families. Only one new model appeared during this decade, the EL2 Aga cooker in 1975. Its design moved away from any previous Aga heat-storage cooker and it looked more like a conventional cooker, built in sheet metal and available in a wide range of colours. The 1980s started in style with Aga's fiftieth anniversary celebration. A lavish birthday party was thrown at the Royal Garden Hotel in London, attended by advertising guru and lifetime Aga supporter David Ogilvy. The company continued to flourish, and its status as something of a national institution was recognised when Prime Minister Margaret Thatcher visited the Coalbrookdale foundry in 1981. Then, in 1985, Aga launched a landmark model – the first electric Aga range cooker, with the two-oven EC2, followed two years later by the four-oven EC4. These new models retained all the traditional features for which Aga cookers were renowned, but for the first time no flue was required, as the cookers vented through a small pipe fanned to the outside. By the end of the decade, more than 8,000 new owners were joining the Aga family each year. In the 1980s the Aga cooker began to feature in romance novels by authors such as Jilly Cooper. This phenomenon gave rise to the expression 'Aga sagas', used to describe this genre of fiction. 'Although we've got a large house, we're always in the kitchen – and we wouldn't be if it weren't for the Aga,' the novelist once said. Mary herself admitted that she was partial to the occasional Aga saga. 'I love Joanna Trollope. I especially liked *The Choir*,' she said in an interview with the *Independent*. 'I like the older ones rather than the more recent ones. I've got them all in a row upstairs. Joanna Trollope does have an Aga herself, of course.'

By the 1990s, the Aga was the oven that anyone who was anyone just had to have. Jan Boxshall's nostalgic *Good Housekeeping* book of the 1990s, *Every Home Should Have One*, described the Aga heat-storage cooker as being the 'epitome of country-kitchen style'. The module was unveiled in 1996 – a conventional electric cooker with traditional Aga styling designed to fit on the left-hand side of the range. Later the same year the companion was introduced – similar to the module, but freestanding. By 1998, both were available with gas hob options.

While the simplicity of the design was what made the Aga so impressive to begin with, over time that simplicity would also prove to be iconic. In 2000, the BBC published a report looking back over the twentieth century. It hand-picked what it considered to be the top three design icons from those 100 years. In first place was the Coca-Cola bottle – with its curvaceous contours, the bottle was instantly recognisable as containing the world's most popular soft drink. In second place was the VW Beetle car, thanks to its bubble-like design that was like no other. And third was the Aga cooker. But as the Aga Cooking website noted: 'Some say you can cook on the engine of a VW Beetle but we leave our roast chicken to the Aga.'

As the cookers became increasingly popular, with exports to the US growing rapidly, Mary's own involvement with the Aga started to develop a life of its own. Having cooked with Agas for most of her adult life, Mary decided to put these skills to good use. It so happened that this decision coincided with that time in her life when she felt she needed to be at home. Having written scores of cookbooks already, Mary suggested that she should write one relating specifically to the Aga. She published *The Aga Book* in 1994 – and it immediately won rave reviews, establishing Mary Berry as the definitive Aga writer, with the *Mail on Sunday*'s *You* magazine boldly declaring: 'Mary Berry is to Aga what Pavarotti is to opera'. The book was filled with scores of recipes for comfort food, including Leek and Stilton Soup and Spiced Treacle Gammon – which serves up to 18 people – plus Mary's various other speciality cake recipes. Ever practical, Mary cleverly made sure that you could cook the recipes without having to own one of the status-symbol cookers, with each recipe including instructions for producing them at normal cooking temperatures in conventional ovens. It also meant the books didn't have a closed-off market and would appeal to anyone who was a fan of Mary's books. Unsurprisingly, they all became best-sellers. More books relating to Aga cooking followed, and she encouraged her loyal PA Lucy to write some too. Mary's original book is still in print and, even today, if you buy an Aga and are worried by the relatively large price tag you can take some comfort in the fact that you'll also be handed a copy of Mary's *The Aga Book* for free. Mary, however, is quite dismissive of the hype that surrounds her involvement with the Aga. 'I'm called the Aga Queen or some such rubbish!' she once said.

In the wake of William's death, Mary was to find another use for her trusty Aga. The devastation wrought by the tragedy understandably contributed to her decision not to continue commuting between London and Buckinghamshire. She decided that, with the help of Lucy, she would host Aga Workshops from home, teaching owners to make the most of the cooker's different features using recipes they could easily replicate in their own kitchens. This would allow her to be at home with her family while continuing to work. And on top of this, it would give her even more time to spend with her beloved Aga.

When asked by Kirsty Young on *Desert Island Discs* whether she made the decision to hold the workshops because she wasn't sure she could 'do something out in the big bad world right now', Mary replied: 'That is exactly how it was. When William died, I … it [wa]s just shattering. And I didn't want to leave Paul, I didn't want to leave the family; I thought, what can I do from home? And having written the Aga book, I knew a lot about it. So I thought nobody is doing a school, I will do it. And we had a steady flow of people and we were always full.'

Mary's cookery school quickly became hugely popular and massively respected. At one point, you had to book up to a year in advance for a spot on one of her courses. Often she would have to cook for as many as 20 people twice a week. Mary tried to keep the numbers limited, however, to allow time for tastings, discussions and a question-and-answer session. The Aga would be used to cook 12 dishes for the class sessions, as well as the lunches for anyone taking part. Adverts for the classes ran in local and national newspapers. One of the first adverts for the courses was placed in the *Independent* newspaper in 1990. Mary penned it herself, and it read: 'The cookery writer Mary Berry gives small classes at her home in Buckinghamshire on working with an Aga cooker. The day-long classes include sessions for new owners, keen bakers and Christmas or dinner party menus.' Email and the web weren't a feature of everyday life back then, so anyone interested in finding out further information was asked to write to Mary at Watercroft. Another advert a few years later, in 1999, in the *London Evening Standard* said: 'Cookery writer Mary Berry runs informal workshops from her Buckinghamshire home. Numbers are limited to 20, to allow time for tastings and a discussion. Lunch is included in the price of £97.52 for one day and £195.05 for two days. A gift card is sent to anyone receiving the workshop as a present.'

In the mid-1990s, five years after the courses were launched, the *Independent*'s Rosie Millard was dispatched to try a course out for herself and write it up as a feature. At the time she had recently acquired an Aga and, by her own admission, was struggling to understand how to make the best of it. A friend, who had recently bought Mary's Aga cookbook, recommended that Rosie sign up for Mary's classes to get to grips with her new toy. She enrolled in Making the Most of the Aga, the most basic of nine Aga courses Mary ran.

Millard took readers through a typical day on one of the courses. Mary started the day by telling the group her aim was to teach people how they could embrace their Aga and use it as efficiently as possible to cook for their family, as well as entertaining friends and relatives – and how to simply enjoy it. Millard observed that Mary was 'looking and sounding rather like a white-haired Julie Andrews'. At first, the participants were gathered in the elegant drawing room at Watercroft for coffee and home-made biscuits, before Mary gave them a tour of her home, finally ending up in the kitchen where the stage had been set for the rest of the day. 'The table has been moved out and 24 chairs arranged in rows before her and her gleaming four-oven monster,' wrote Millard. 'Two women in aprons cluck around behind her. Throughout the day, they provide things such as egg white or chopped parsley with silent efficiency; but Mrs Berry is the star.'

All sorts of different people would attend Mary's classes – from mothers with large families to City traders. The differing backgrounds of the people taking her courses was something Mary embraced. She said in an interview with *The Times* that some of her clients returned up to 14 times, and that the vast majority weren't stay-at-home mothers whose life was dedicated to baking. 'My people at workshops tell me all sorts of stories,' said Mary. 'Like, "I don't mind my husband going but I don't want to lose the Aga." Or, if they are getting divorced, "It's bad enough losing him but not the Aga, too."'

During the course, Millard was taught to make Yorkshire puddings, as well as a roast, a cake, a casserole, a lemon Swiss roll, a treacle bake, salmon in filo pastry, roast fillet of pork, meringues and crème brûlée... before moving on to the titan of baking dishes – the quiche. 'Still, Mrs Berry's technique is nothing if not confidence-building,' wrote

Millard. Mary gave the class all manner of advice. Everything from how to line a roasting tin with foil to mastering the difficult task of making pastry that didn't crumble. Mary also taught them how to avoid her ultimate faux-pas – the soggy bottom, which would later come to become one of her buzz phrases on the *Great British Bake Off*. After the morning session, Mary would then invite her students into the dining room for lunch, where they would chat away the afternoon, exchanging stories about their lives and experiences with their Aga while sipping white wine and eating spicy chicken fricassée. But while the Aga was undoubtedly a revolutionary piece of kitchen equipment both in the way it cooked and its multi-faceted uses aside from food preparation, Millard realised there was another reason why Mary managed to make it so popular. The food she cooked wasn't elaborate nouveau cuisine, but honest fare that filled a spot. She said: 'Perhaps the popularity of the day is not due to an Aga being a terrifying piece of equipment needing hours of tuition to master, but to a sort of culinary comfort factor. The course propounds the delights of old-fashioned, familiar things such as Kenwood Chefs and mashed potato, and there is no worrying trip into the language of haute cuisine.'

As Mary's workshops became famous around the UK, their popularity surged, with Aga lovers clamouring for a place. In the introduction to a new edition of *The Aga Book*, Mary said that owning one of the ovens gave people a sense of inclusion and that it was 'like joining the best club in the country ... when you meet another Aga owner it is like discovering an instant friend. The Aga gives you a welcome. It's warm and it's ready,' she wrote. 'Those who knock it are used to conventional cookers and have never actually taken the trouble to understand it.'

And if anything demonstrated how owning an Aga had become such an exclusive club, it was a piece in the *Daily Telegraph* in 2009. The newspaper went on a quest to work out who in Britain owned the oldest Aga. In conjunction with Aga, the broadsheet asked readers to find the earliest example of the classic stove still in domestic use and to include any unusual stories about it. Agas had become known for their durability. These weren't cookers that would simply be used for a few years until the next kitchen refurbishment. Many would last decades and continue to operate for more than 50 years. And so to celebrate this longevity, as well as the company's 300th anniversary, the competition was launched. Thousands entered with all sorts of weird, wonderful and colourful stories about the history of their own heat-storage cookers which demonstrated the rich cultural history that the Aga brought with it. 'Osbert Hicks from St Agnes on the Isles of Scilly, for example, has a 1937 Aga installed by his parents that is still in daily use,' wrote *Daily Telegraph* journalist Adam Edwards. 'John Fowler's 1938 model that is thundering away in Essex has survived both bombs and doodlebugs. Karen Hamilton from Moray in Scotland has a 60-year-old machine that was completely flooded in the fifties. It was soon back in service, but the saucepan of soup that had been cooking on the hot plate was not found for another two weeks.'

Meanwhile another reader, Nicky Gill, from Dorset, remembered her Aunt Maidie's Aga being used for purposes quite different to cooking during the 1940s. 'She was a matronly figure with a booming voice and a magnificent bosom who would return from bracing winter walks and beg a few moments alone in the kitchen,' wrote Nicky. 'If the kitchen door was ajar we could see Auntie Maidie raise her jumper, lean over the hot plates and emit a deep sigh while uttering the words "ah, one of life's great pleasures".'

Many of the Agas entered for the competition had been found hidden behind false walls or cupboards. "When we moved into our house in 1976 we asked the builders to remove the kitchen wall cupboards," wrote Mrs S Hindmarch from Danbury, Essex. "When they pulled them away from the wall they found a beautifully cleaned Aga with all tools wrapped in oil cloths placed inside the oven. It must have been there for at least 18 years."

But the oldest Aga belonged to the Hett family, from Sussex. In 1932, the family decided it was about time to join the world of modern cooking and subsequently had the state-of-the-art foreign cooker installed in their home. It was the same year, the *Daily Telegraph* noted, that the celebrated author Aldous Huxley released his international best-selling book *Brave New World*. Indeed, the Hett family did join the brave new world of cooking ... and still have the evidence to prove it. Even in 2009, some 77 years after the Aga was first installed, 80-year-old Stewart Hett was still basking in the joys of the very same heat-storage cooker. He was still living in the same house that his parents had bought and was still cooking on the exact same stove. He duly won the award for owning the oldest continuous working domestic Aga, after Aga expert Richard Maggs confirmed that the Hett Aga was a genuine 1932 stove. 'It is perhaps not in the best of nick,' Edwards wrote in the piece. 'A side-oven door broke and was substituted with a bit of rough steel. At some stage the old cream enamel hot-plate lids must have been replaced by aluminium jobs and the whole machine now looks as if it would only work properly if it was overseen by the cartoonist Heath. And yet it potters on regardless, with the same reliability and simplicity of purpose as a Zippo [cigarette lighter].' The Hett family's Aga was later moved and installed in the reception area of Aga's Coalbrookdale foundry.

But it wasn't just Brits who embraced the Aga. America was discovering a love for the double-plated stove, and Hollywood stars were apparently snapping up the fashionable cooker. Whereas it cost around £4,000 for a mid-range model (including installation) in the UK, the price tag in the US was an eye-watering $15,000 (approximately £10,000). Even so, in 1997, 300 had been installed across the whole of the US – that's the equivalent of six in each state. The trend appeared to be started by the prestigious *TIME* magazine, which dedicated a three-page feature to the Great British Stove. Back in Britain the *Daily Express* was reporting that movie stars including Julia Roberts and Dustin Hoffman had invested in the stove. 'Forget fashion or fragrance, the latest must-have in America is nothing less than an old-fashioned British cooker,' the *Daily Express* said. 'Americans covet our history because they haven't any of their own, and the closest way they can attain this is to buy British.'

And as the popularity of the Aga grew in America, word reached the other side of the pond about Mary's courses. She was even asked to fly to the States to deliver some of her classes. 'I don't know about Hollywood,' said Mary in *The Times*. 'But I went to America last year to do Aga Workshops – Atlanta, New York and around – and America is the perfect place because if you are rich there you have two houses and one is in the mountains, and what better welcome can you get than from an Aga?' Americans were also starting to fly to England to take Mary's classes at Watercroft.

Other than Hollywood, other celebrities were soon celebrating the joys of the Aga, including Rick Stein, John Nettles and Robbie Coltrane. Sharon Stone even suggested that her Aga would be the first thing she'd try to rescue if her house caught fire. The model Jodie Kidd added her backing, saying: 'I was brought up around the Aga. It has always symbolised for me such wonderful things: good food, warmth and protection.'

Poetry entertainer Pam Ayres, who lives at Poulton, near Cirencester, said she had been an early convert to the Aga for many of the same reasons that Mary enjoyed using it. 'I love the Aga,' she said in an interview. 'It really is a family friend. I feel very affectionate towards it. It's always there when you need it. I have it on all year round. People come into the kitchen and automatically lounge against it. It's a warm focal point. The dog and I always sit with our backs against it. Lovely! The drying rack over it has seen some history – drying all my sons' clothes, from tiny baby bits to huge rugby shirts. And when we tried our hand at farming, with a herd of 50 sheep, it saved the life of a lamb. It was weak and dying and we put it in the bottom oven of the Aga and it brought it back to life. I also dry herbs, flowers and kidney beans in it, iron my tea towels on it and raise yeast for bread in it. Without the Aga I'd be raising yeast in the airing cupboard and cranking up the oven to the right temperature every time I wanted to make dinner. I don't know what I'd do without it.'

Meanwhile Jamie Oliver admitted he too was a fan of the Aga, after he got one just a few years ago in his family home. With his wife Jools and four children to look after, he says it gets put to good and regular use. Finding their dream house was exciting, and installing an Aga in the kitchen was the cherry on the cake, especially as Jools had wanted one since the couple got married. Besides, a stainless-steel appliance wasn't going to look right. 'I don't believe there's anything you can't cook on an Aga. The way I cook these days is, if I'm going to have breakfast, I've got about four minutes to do it. So I do need that immediate heat. If I have to wait for a grill to pre-heat – even if it's just five minutes – then it's impossible: I'm late. So it's a lifestyle thing as well.' Jamie drew parallels between people who learn how to get the most out of their Aga by really understanding cooking, and committed vegetarians, believing that serious vegetarians who love food are good cooks 'because they have to duck and dive a little bit to get around the fact they're not eating meat.'

Mary's workshops ran for some 16 years – a length of time she could never have imagined when she first came up with the idea. In total, she welcomed over 12,000 into her home at Watercroft for classes. But as Mary got older and her media schedule became ever busier, balancing the classes with the rest of her career became difficult, so she made the tough decision to give up teaching them. But, realising there was still a demand for the classes, she came up with a plan. Her long-time assistant Lucy had always lent a hand during her classes, and it seemed like the perfect idea to pass the baton to her. So, while Mary has retired from teaching, a new generation of Aga lovers is being taught by Lucy, who now runs the workshops. Writing on her website, Mary said: 'I can honestly say I have enjoyed each day, thanks to our guests and the support from Lucy and the home team. Alas, the time came for me to slow down a little and spend more time with Paul and the family. I will still be doing bits and bobs, TV, radio, and some demonstrations around the country so you may see me on your travels, but the Aga Workshops at Watercroft have finished, so it's now over to Lucy. Lucy has been with me the whole journey and we have loved every second; we have been privileged to meet and become friends with so many Aga owners over the years. Lucy will still be working with me part-time, helping me with my TV and radio programmes, books and so forth but she will also be doing her own books, writing and demonstrations. Lucy will continue the Aga Workshops in the future – travelling to Aga shops and cookery schools around the country ... Thank you for all your wonderful support.'

But while the support for Mary's courses was undeniable, the Aga's history has also been peppered with some controversies. Feminists claimed the stove was forcing women to feel chained to their kitchen. 'The Aga backlash has begun,' declared *The Times* in 1996. 'A campaign against the hearty, hearthy home cooking of Delia Smith is to be launched today. The Cooks Off Club aims to get women out of the kitchen, and its launch has already boiled over into a sizzling row about the merits of the kitchen stove.' The anti-Aga movement was led by the writer Sue Limb, who used Radio 4's *Woman's Hour* as her soapbox. She poked fun at women who were 'stove slaves' and the programme was overwhelmed by the response. 'We realised that there are an awful lot of people who hate cooking but are afraid to admit it,' the programme's producer, Jane O'Rourke, said at the time. 'We will be asking people to send in ideas on how to avoid cooking and to re-educate people to enjoy raw food.'

Mary was, understandably, dismissive of the campaign and backed her beloved stove with her usual loyalty. 'People who haven't got Agas are probably leading the campaign. But it's not just cooking: it's warmth and comfort and somewhere to dry the tea towels. The Aga is a way of life.'

Perhaps on a more serious note, environmental concerns were being raised about the appliance itself. Campaigners have pointed out the cooker's lack of energy efficiency, and the facts are hard to argue with. According to Aga's own figures, a four-oven model gets through either 13 gallons of diesel oil, 15 gallons of kerosene, 24.5 therms of gas or 270kwh of electricity per week. Edinburgh University geoscientist Dr Dave Reay, who wrote the book *Climate Change Begins At Home*, said in a *Daily Telegraph* article: 'It's an energy hog. A normal oven gets through just 10kwh of electricity a week and produces 4kg of carbon dioxide (CO_2), whereas a four-door Aga gets through 270kwh and produces 108kg of CO_2. So it's more than 25 times more polluting in terms of CO_2. That said, it does give extra space heating, but as this is localised – so probably not in the places it's really needed – the savings on heating fuel are not massive.'

In short, the smallest two-oven gas Aga, when being

used in the simplest way for cooking, rather than water heating or central heating, uses as much gas in one week as a standard gas oven or hob would do during the course of nine months.

Before he became Prime Minister, David Cameron was involved in his own Aga saga. It was revealed that he had one at his constituency home in Chipping Norton, Oxford – and the environmentalists were up in arms, cheered on by the media. However, his spokeswoman was quick to point out that it wasn't through his choosing that he had come to own one, saying: 'He didn't actually choose it himself, he inherited it from the previous occupants. He also says that his Aga is turned off most of the time, so in fact it isn't too bad for the environment.' Cameron's critics maintained that this was not possible – the whole point of an Aga is that it stays switched on the whole time.

Cameron's cause wasn't helped by Dominic Loehnis, a long-standing friend of the Tory leader, when he told the *Daily Telegraph* in October 2005: 'The smell of the Cameron household is of bacon in the Aga.'

But the Aga company has gone to great lengths to put a positive spin on all the negative PR. Aga says that one of the cooker's great eco-virtues is the fact that the stove is made from recycled cast iron. Laura James, editor of *Aga* magazine, said: 'It's the original recycled product. Up to 70 per cent of each oven is recycled material. You might have to buy two or three conventional cookers in the course of your lifetime, but you will only ever need to buy one Aga.'

Aga did, however, come up with a 'biofuel-enabled' model, perhaps in an attempt to improve their environmental credentials. Rather than using fossil fuels with finite supplies such as oil and diesel, the company said that the new models used material 'derived from recently living organisms or their metabolic by-products, such as cow manure'. The only snag was that, at the time of production, the biofuel wasn't available – and so the new cookers, which were significantly more expensive, costing up to £7,425, still had to run on oil and diesel.

But while the Aga's lack of energy efficiency has become a sizeable story over recent years, some owners have come out fighting. They insist that the Aga helps to create a far more energy-efficient home, owing to the fact that Aga doesn't simply cook, but can replace radiators and central heating systems. It can be used to dry clothes, instead of a tumble dryer. It is not simply an oven or a hob, and so, they say, it should not be compared to one when it comes to energy consumption. Writing a blog entitled 'In defence of the Aga' on the *Guardian* website, one fan wrote: 'The main argument against the Aga is that it's environmentally unsound, and this is often tied to it being representative of a smug middle-class lifestyle … Buying an Aga changed my life. Because the oven is on all the time, I cook more from scratch, so we eat better, and our cold Victorian flat is a healthier and more pleasant environment. To paraphrase Princess Diana, there are three of us in this family: myself, my daughter and the cream, black and chrome piece of heavyweight design that provides the heart and hearth of our home.'

For her part, Mary didn't like the sound of the eco-friendly model of the Aga. 'I'm going to wait until I hear good reports of it,' she said. 'Besides, there are always ways in which people can use their conventional Agas more wisely and economically – like not leaving the tops open and letting the heat out.' Neither is Mary particularly fussed when it comes to the 'green' issues surrounding her beloved stove. On the issue of the Aga having a poor environmental footprint more generally, Mary wasn't convinced it was a reason not to use the stove. 'I like to be green on other things and do what I can, but I'm not so concerned about the Aga,' Mary said to the *Guardian*.

Aside from the controversies, business doesn't appear to be booming as much as it once was, and Aga's profits have dropped in recent years. In January 2012, the *Daily Mail* reported that the company had experienced a 3 per cent dip in annual revenues, claiming that performance was as good as could be expected given tough market conditions. Revenues were down to £251 million after a particularly tough end to 2011. The paper said that, despite the drop, the firm still anticipated decent profits when it delivered its full year results, as by focusing on markets such as the US and France, it was in a good position to weather the global economic downturn, so had a positive outlook for 2012 and beyond.

But whether or not the Aga remains as in fashion as it once was, Mary's loyalty to the product and its brand has remained unwavering. Like a trusted friend, she refuses to abandon it. She was chosen as the official face of Aga and in January 2012 opened a new Aga store in Ringwood, Hampshire, as part of her role. At the grand opening, town crier and Aga demonstrator Diane Van Bueren cooked Mary Berry recipes all day for guests to taste. Meanwhile, Mary cut the ribbon and opened the shop before chatting to guests and signing copies of her new book, *Family*

Sunday Lunches. Her Aga cookbooks continue to sell and, it seems, there is no end in sight for Mary's winning relationship with her stove.

CHAPTER 7

FROM BAKING TO BROADCASTING

By the late 1970s, Mary had positioned herself as a formidable cookery writer. *The Hamlyn All Colour Cook Book* had become a best-seller and she had released a handful of other titles which were also flying off the shelves. Mary was being spoken about as the next big thing in cooking. And as the buzz surrounding her and her work grew, TV producers started to notice her too. Constantly on the lookout for the next cook to appear on their shows, they started to compete to try to sign her up for their programmes. The first that came calling was the ITV show *Afternoon Plus* – a teatime chat show fronted by Judith Chalmers OBE. Judith, then in her forties, was breaking through as a major TV presenter. She had already presented the ballroom dancing competition programme *Come Dancing* for the BBC from 1961 to 1965. This was a huge primetime hit that would later be reinvented with a celebrity twist as *Strictly Come Dancing* nearly forty years later. She had also become a star on the radio, presenting two major BBC radio shows, *Family Favourites* and *Woman's Hour*. Judith would later become best known for presenting the holiday getaway show *Wish You Were Here...?* during the 1980s on ITV. The programme saw her jetting around the globe to seek out the best deals on vacations. Judith herself was often featured in the papers for her habit of wearing bikinis as she fronted the hit show. But for the time being she had broken through to the popular daytime market, and was already getting good ratings with her new show.

Afternoon Plus had a magazine format that mixed interviews with lifestyle segments including gardening, fashion tips – and cookery. Thames Television, who produced the show, have often been seen as having changed the face of daytime TV with the programme, by bringing what one commentator called 'the art of intelligent interviewing to a wide and growing audience'. *Afternoon Plus* was seen by some as a smarter alternative to the BBC's more accessible *Pebble Mill at One*, which was nevertheless hugely popular with the target audience of housewives, students and those recovering from illness in bed at home, and would often get viewing figures of 6 million – a huge coup for a lunchtime show. But *Afternoon Plus* came out punching, determined to be a viable rival. Impressively, the show managed to secure a string of A-list stars to appear on the studio sofa, including actresses Sophia Loren and Helen Mirren, as well as the hugely successful soul diva Nina Simone.

But now the people behind *Afternoon Plus* wanted a regular guest to appear on the show to discuss cookery. If they were to capture the housewives' market, it was vital that a segment be dedicated to the kitchen. And Mary seemed like the perfect solution. She was to share her culinary secrets – her dos and don'ts for the kitchen – and respond to viewer questions about recipes on a regular basis. So, when Mary was approached by the show's producers, she accepted. But it wasn't without trepidation. For Mary, the prospect of appearing on television was a daunting one. Having worked as a cook all her life, she knew her way around the kitchen, but not the TV studio. While she could write endlessly about cooking in the comfort of her own home, performing in front of a TV audience of millions was another matter entirely.

Luckily, Judith became a good friend and showed her the ropes. Any nerves Mary might have had quickly disappeared, as Judith provided a friendly face among the hive of activity that was the TV studio. 'In the early days of my career, my first cooking programmes were with Judith Chalmers,' Mary told the *Scotsman*. 'She really helped me to enjoy the whole experience, and showed me how to smile naturally on television.' Mary was such a hit that she ended up appearing on the show regularly for no fewer than seven series. And *Afternoon Plus* would prove to be the start of a glittering TV career for Mary, as she went on to front her own shows before landing her coveted judging role on *GBBO*.

However, Mary says that Judith had one piece of advice that she has carried with her through all the other TV programmes she has since been a part of. 'When I started doing television on Judith Chalmers's show *Afternoon Plus*, she told me to forget about the audience and imagine I was talking to one person who was doing the ironing,' Mary said in an interview with the *Daily Mail*. 'That was one of the best pieces of advice I was ever given.'

Bizarrely enough, it was the same advice that her boss at the PR firm Bensons had given her when she was concerned about writing recipes for the first time for *Housewife* magazine ... just to approach it as if she was having a chat. The technique worked wonders on screen, just as it had in print. It was this conversational style that made Mary a hit with the viewers and secured her even more TV work.

Clips from Mary on the show were recently uploaded from the Thames Television archive onto video streaming website YouTube. Looking at them today gives a glimpse into how cookery on daytime TV shows has since evolved, yet in other ways it has very much stayed the same. Under the title 'Cooking retro style', Mary is seen alongside Judith cooking a stuffed shoulder of lamb and then later a pâté. Her easy-going, conversational style is plain to see as she wears a multicoloured patchwork shirt and flowing, ankle-length black dress. She talks openly to viewers about her own life, peppering her segments with anecdotes from Watercroft. In one clip she speaks about how she is growing parsley in her garden, what she and her family had for Sunday lunch and the fact that her children are 'conkering' – playing with horse chestnuts threaded with string – causing her to run out of string for cooking in her home kitchen.

Mary's asides, like: 'It's a real sticky job today, isn't it Judy?' keep the tone of the segment lighthearted and enjoyable. Yet it's easy to see that the segment is a lot more formal than cookery shows are these days, as well as being far slower paced. Whereas today measurements of ingredients and the precise technical procedures for making dishes are often swept aside in favour of personality-driven, quick-to-cook recipes (with the nitty-gritty available on the programme's website or in the tie-in book), back then Mary went through each stage of cooking the dish methodically and slowly, lingering over every element of the recipe in order to encourage as many people as possible to give it a go themselves at home.

But the segment's set, of a kitchen against the backdrop of a domestic environment with fine china lined up on wooden shelving, is similar to what we would expect to see today, with the presenter – in this case Judith – standing alongside as Mary carries out the recipe.

Mary's appearances underline the somewhat seismic changes that have occurred in TV cookery, which have been noted by critics and commentators over the intervening years. 'Berry comes from a calmer age of television cookery, where the food, not the personality of the presenter, was what counted,' the feature writer Elfreda Pownall noted in *Stella* magazine, before adding: 'And helping people to cook better at home was the aim.'

When Mary first started in TV, cookery shows were, in essence, about bringing cookbooks to life. But by the turn of the twenty-first century, cookery writing had changed. No longer was it just about the step-by-step guides to cooking, but more in-depth questions were being asked by the consumer. Was the produce organic? How could you impress at a dinner party? Was the dish low in fat? Did it have a low GI? What ingredients could you substitute if some weren't available?

'Cooking shows have taught us, changed us and changed with us,' wrote author Kathleen Collins in her book *Watching What We Eat: The Evolution of Television Cooking Shows*. 'At the beginning of the twenty-first century, they have evolved to satisfy our yearning for quality, affordable, environmentally and health conscious, easy to prepare yet sophisticated food. And while many viewers may not have the time to execute the lessons nor the money to afford the high-end ingredients or appliances used by cooking-show hosts, these shows prevail because everyone eats, knows something about food, and can relate to the endeavour.'

The cultural and social importance of cookery shows should not be underestimated. They have helped transform cookery from a drudge, a necessity and a chore for housewives around the world into a creative, exciting and enjoyable activity. Writing in the *New York Times*, Michael Pollan elaborated on this as he discussed the 2009 Hollywood film starring Academy Award winner Meryl Streep, *Julie & Julia*. The film chronicles the early career of Julia Child, one of the first popular American TV chefs. Pollan argues that Child set about bringing this sea change in the world's view of cooking as she started out in TV in the 1960s, at almost exactly the same time as Mary was beginning her own broadcasting career. Pollan said: 'That learning to cook could lead an American woman to success of any kind would have seemed utterly implausible in 1949; that it is so thoroughly plausible 60 years later owes everything to Julia Child's legacy ... chefs have been welcomed into the repertory company of American celebrity and cooking has become a broadly appealing *mise en scène* in which success stories can plausibly be set and played out.' Citing the Food Network and a hit show on that channel called *The Next Food Network Star*, he said it was amazing that we live in a culture where thousands of 20- and 30-

somethings compete eagerly to become recognised for their culinary prowess.

When Mary began her TV career in the late 1960s, it would have been almost impossible to imagine that, years later, there would be a whole TV channel dedicated to cookery shows. The Food Network launched in the US in 1993, before coming to the UK and Ireland as a satellite channel in 2009. It screens wall-to-wall cookery shows of all descriptions – reality programmes, documentaries and step-by-step classes for any skill level, from novices to masterchefs.

The popularity of the Food Network is such that it's now available in almost 100 million American homes and often gets ratings above and beyond any of the more so-called serious news channels. Food was suddenly seen as something that could delight, rather than just something you ate for breakfast, lunch and dinner. It had the power to entertain both on screen and on the viewer's plate. 'Cooking shows also benefit from the fact that food itself is – by definition – attractive to the humans who eat it,' wrote Pollan. Techniques such as food styling, where a whole host of tricks is deployed to make dishes look appetising in front of the camera, appeal to our physiological and psychological responses to seeing food. So a slow-motion cascade of glistening red cherries or a tongue of flame lapping at a slab of meat on the grill catches our eye. 'Food shows are the campfires in the deep cable forest,' said Pollan, 'drawing us like hungry wanderers to their flames.'

In recent years, the number of people holding dinner parties in the UK has shot up. Retail analysts Conlumino carried out a survey which showed that 30 per cent of respondents said they'd thrown a dinner party in the six months leading up to May 2012 – a 12 per cent increase on the previous year. The rise of TV cookery is said to be a major contributing factor to this statistic. The process of holding dinner parties has become so popular that TV cookery shows have started to reflect this. Perhaps inspired by the likes of Jamie, Delia or Mary, Channel 4's *Come Dine With Me* sees groups of four or five strangers living near each other in some part of the UK treating each other to dinner parties, with the attendees giving each other scores out of 10. The contestant who emerges at the end of the week with the highest score takes home a cash prize of £1,000. The show became a cult hit thanks to its winning combination of reality, fly-on-the-wall-style TV coupled with cookery. It's clear that, over the years, cookery shows have evolved to meet viewers' interests and, indeed, tastes.

With the changing landscape of cookery shows, programmes have had to be revamped and reinvented to stay on trend. But not everyone has appreciated these changes. BBC2 – the channel that would later screen Mary on the *Great British Bake Off* – would do just that with its long-running hit *MasterChef*. While it helped to completely rejuvenate the show's ratings, which had always been stable, it did not go down so well with the former host, Loyd Grossman, who spoke openly about his dislike of some of the changes. Grossman, who presented the show for 10 years, quit in 2000 after he was told the show would be moved from its usual Sunday afternoon slot on BBC1 to a Tuesday night on BBC2 in an attempt to capture a wider audience. Grossman said at the time: 'The programme is a dumb thing and I don't want to be involved.' Celebrity chef Gary Rhodes, who had much success behind him as a cookery book writer and TV presenter, was brought in as Grossman's replacement, but only for one series. Four years later, the show was given a completely new lease of life with former grocer Gregg Wallace and restaurateur John Torode taking the reins. It is once again a big hit, but Grossman was still dissatisfied. He objected to what he felt was the presenters' 'aggressive' on-screen style and poked fun at Wallace's catchphrase: 'Cooking doesn't get tougher than this.' Grossman added: 'It's like *Lock, Stock and Two Smoking Barrels*.'

With TV cookery shows being constantly updated and becoming ever more popular, especially competitive formats such as *MasterChef* and later Paul and Mary's *Great British Bake Off*, it seemed only a matter of time before the world's number one TV mogul wanted a slice of the pie. Simon Cowell is the force behind huge reality hits *Pop Idol*, *The X Factor* and the *Got Talent* franchises, which have since been bought by scores of other countries around the world. Seeing the power of cookery to entertain, Cowell has now made his first moves into the world of TV cookery with a new show. Screened by the BBC's main rival, ITV, *Food Glorious Food* involves a team of culinary experts touring the country in search of the best family recipe, with the winning dish sold nationwide in supermarket chain Marks & Spencer. Speaking about his new project, Cowell insisted it was 'not a show for snobs'. Food shows, he insisted, should be accessible to everyone. He wanted *Food Glorious Food* to celebrate simple, everyday cooking, adding: 'I like home food, I love it. My mum's roast potatoes. Shepherd's pie. Cornish pasties. I want stuff like that on the show.' Never one to miss a trick, the first judge Cowell signed up for the new show was none other than ... Loyd Grossman. Cookery shows appear to have entered a new realm, where it's not just about the food – competition and drama are just as vital ingredients as the dishes that are being prepared.

Perhaps the beauty of Mary's TV career is that she hasn't had to change with the times to remain a success. The simplicity of her recipes and overall approach have a kind of timelessness – something that has allowed her to maintain a loyal and ever-growing following. As a result of her appearances on *Afternoon Plus*, not only did she win fans among the viewers, but among the show's makers at Thames Television, too. They decided they wanted Mary to feature regularly in their programming – not just on *Afternoon Plus*. This led to them offering her a series of shows in which she would be the star. It was a huge crossover moment for Mary. No longer would she be featuring on someone else's show; she would be presenting her own. In total she hosted seven series for Thames Television. The format didn't alter greatly from what viewers were used to on *Afternoon Plus*. Mary would guide the audience slowly, step by step, through recipes that could easily be prepared at home in the viewers' own kitchens. Decades before Delia Smith presented her *Summer Collection* from the kitchen of her Norfolk cottage, or Nigella welcomed the cameras into her West London townhouse to cook dishes from her latest book, the backdrop to these shows starring Mary was often her own home at Watercroft.

But there was a particular subtle difference that, once again, marked Mary out as a true pioneer. For the first time, her cookery books were released to tie with her TV series. It had rarely been done with any success before Mary. But for the first time she released *Television Cook Book* in October 1979, to coincide with one of her Thames Television series. The simplicity of the title shows just how new a concept it was. There was no need for a fancy title – the very fact that it was a cookbook linked with a TV show seemed unique and novel enough to market it successfully. Television companies and publishers alike would quickly start seeing the benefits of this combined approach. Fans of Mary's cookbooks would tune in to her TV series, and fans of her TV series would now start buying her cookbooks. It's a format that has been replicated both here in the UK and around the world ever since. Nowadays celebrity cooks and chefs, from James Martin to Lorraine Pascale, rarely have a cookery series without a book to tie in with it. Once again Mary had proved that she was a trailblazer.

And after a long and successful run of series with Thames Television, the BBC also wanted a slice of the Mary Berry pie – they too recruited her for a string of series. These included *Mary Berry at Home* and *Mary Berry's Ultimate Cakes*. Both series had eight episodes and were all filmed at her family home in Buckinghamshire. But even though these series were filmed some years after Mary had first started to feature on TV regularly, she always kept her shows simple. In *Ultimate Cakes*, for example, she dedicated a whole episode to making scones. Mary's recipe for these light, fluffy delights has since become legendary and there was a public outcry when Paul Hollywood's recipe was used instead of Mary's in one episode of the *Great British Bake Off*. Another episode in the series was dedicated to baking cakes involving fresh fruit, including a Raspberry Meringue Roulade. Meanwhile, later in the series, a programme focused on baking for fundraising events and also 'fast bakes' – cakes that could be easily prepared by those who didn't have much time on their hands. In contrast, other cooks such as Nigella Lawson would later successfully give viewers the confidence to tackle more opulent recipes.

But while Mary was becoming a star in her own right, she would also feature on another long-running series. *Houseparty* became a huge hit on daytime TV from the late 1960s to the 1980s. It had a similar format to ITV1's *Loose Women*, a show that rose to great popularity during the 2000s. This panel show consists of four women discussing topical issues, interviewing guests and, often, being outspoken about the news stories of the day. It has made celebrities of the panellists and is often seen as the 'crown jewel' in ITV1's current daytime scheduling. It was based on the format of another successful panel show in the US, called *The View*, which became popular with housewives who felt they could empathise with the similarly-aged female panellists. But some 30 years before these programmes, *Houseparty* appears to have paved the way, with production company Southern seeing the potential in the format. One website, TV Cream, recalled the show fondly, saying: 'Here was one independent afternoon banker that was as unglamorous as the medium ever got. August 19, 1969 saw Southern's first colour transmissions hit the air with the orange and brown finery of the *Houseparty* kitchen-cum-lounge, a modernist, open-plan affair complete with Formica surfaces and hessian wall-weave, lovingly re-created in Southampton's Studio 1. Punctuated by the occasional guest-introducing doorbell ("I wonder who that could be?"), the mumsy Ann Ladbury and the patrician former model Cherry Marshall (later joined by daughter Sarah) led a genteel, open-ended stream of chat among half a dozen personable housewives over the Poole pottery chinaware, with the viewer as casual eavesdropper.'

The concept of the viewer 'eavesdropping' on the women was central to the show's whole premise. The show would go off air with the ladies still talking and would often start with them mid-sentence. These were ladies who were going about their business and the viewers were just 'dropping in'. As with all daytime TV, cookery was an integral part of the show. The producers needed someone who could fit in with the conversational style of the programme while also convivially pulling together a recipe in the 'house's' makeshift kitchen. As Mary's profile as a popular TV cook continued to rise, she seemed like the obvious choice. She was picked and took part in a few series alongside her other TV and radio commitments, while also writing more and more cookbooks. Sadly the show's run eventually came to an end, leaving Mary to focus on other projects. Nevertheless it is still fondly remembered by TV buffs as being the precursor to big shows like *The View* and *Loose Women* – even if the very heated debates sometimes seen today were strictly off the menu then. The TV Cream website continued: 'Instead, knitwear, cookery and macramé were the order of the day, the raciest it ever got being when bras were tried on for size (over the twin-sets, of course). Sadly, even this seemingly non-stop cosy camaraderie had to come to an end when Southern lost its franchise ... and the final programme was appropriately emotional – no tears or anything of course, that wasn't the *Houseparty* way, just a few rather touching goodbyes and one last round of tea. Well, they didn't like to make a fuss.'

It's fair to say that Mary had plenty of experience under her belt when it came to live television, even by the end of the 1970s. With her relaxed style she appeared a natural, and it was no wonder that more and more cookery show producers came knocking for years to come. However, Mary revealed that she never fully felt comfortable taking part in shows that weren't pre-recorded. In fact, she went so far as to suggest that she almost had a phobia of taking part in live television programmes. In an interview with the *Scotsman*, she was asked what kept her up at night, to which she replied: 'The knowledge that I have to cook on live television the next day.' Despite her obvious experience both in the kitchen and in front of the camera, by her own admission combining the two would never be something with which she would be totally at ease. And the fact that Mary remains a little daunted by live television despite her obvious ability is probably part of what continues to endear her to both viewers and cookery show producers alike.

Indeed, Mary has achieved something else over the years that has eluded many female TV stars – career longevity. Despite her age, she's still working at a high level. Arguably, real TV superstardom only came for Mary in 2010 when she was picked for the *Great British Bake Off*, aged 75. In Britain, she is probably one of the few exceptions to the apparent rule that older women can't make it in TV. Much has been written about a perceived ageism in the TV industry in the UK – especially towards women. High-profile stars have often spoken out about being sidelined; feeling as though they have been replaced by younger presenters who are more more fresh-faced but with less experience. Things appeared to come to a head in 2009, when the longtime presenter of BBC1's *Countryfile*, Miriam O'Reilly, was dropped from the show. She successfully sued the BBC for age discrimination, saying at the start of her court case that she could no longer watch the programme after being axed from it, as it was too emotionally painful. During the hearing, former BBC1 controller Jay Hunt was called as a witness, and O'Reilly accused her of ageism and sexism and alleged that she 'hated women'. In January 2011, the day after Hunt began working at Channel 4, O'Reilly's claims of age discrimination and victimisation were upheld. She has since been vocal about what she believes is an endemic culture of age discrimination in the TV industry. She said that 'the public want to see women who aren't young, blonde and buxom, but who know what they're talking about', in an interview with the *Sunday Mirror*. 'I don't think having wrinkles is offensive,' she added. 'Being dropped from the programme, I believe because of my age and sex, really affected my confidence.' Meanwhile Carol Smillie, once the Queen of DIY shows who presented the primetime hit *Changing Rooms* on BBC1 during the 1990s and early 2000s, also bemoaned the lack of work for female stars over 50. She too insisted she had been pushed to one side in order to make way for more youthful presenters. 'TV is crazy … it's not the real world. It's such a fickle, shallow world sometimes,' she told the *Sunday Mirror*. 'I was young, fresh-faced and in demand … and now I'm older and I don't get so much work. Well, quelle surprise! There's ageism in TV and there always has been. There's a dark side to the industry that's not attractive.'

Others agree. Ex-newsreader Anna Ford, 68, slammed BBC bosses for not doing enough to put older women on screen. And in 2009 the hugely experienced Arlene Phillips was at the centre of a media storm after her contract as a judge on BBC1's ballroom hit *Strictly Come Dancing* was terminated. At the time Arlene was 66, with a long career as a choreographer behind her, and she was swiftly replaced by thirtysomething Alesha Dixon, who had only taken up ballroom dancing when she had competed on the show and won it the previous year.

The rise of reality TV, some have suggested, has been the precursor to the end of women working into their old age in TV land. 'Reality TV has a lot to answer for ... fame is instant,' Smillie continued in her interview in the *Sunday Mirror*. 'I'm sounding really old now, like a dinosaur, but kids don't wait for anything now. Once you had to earn your stripes. But it's not like that anymore. I think it's sad. We've become so used to seeing a pretty young woman co-host with a father-figure-type older guy. It wouldn't be acceptable in any other profession. The proof of the pudding is in the eating and these people don't last because they don't have any real experience. There's a lot of back-slapping and people thinking they're fabulous.'

For her part, Mary is defiant. She insists she has never encountered ageism in television work. In fact, Mary thinks quite the opposite – it was reality TV of sorts that got her back on to the screen in the form of *GBBO*. 'I'm always reading about women being dropped from TV shows for being too old,' she said in an interview with the *Daily Mail*. 'I find it rather bemusing because I'm older than all of them. I think it's good to have all ages on television – you need someone who has been in the business of baking a long time, don't you?'

But others have suggested that the only way for female TV stars to survive is, in fact, to make sure they look younger. And if that means cosmetic surgery, so be it. The tough-talking host of BBC1's consumer show *Watchdog* and quiz show *Weakest Link* Anne Robinson has often spoken of how she has embraced surgical facelifts wholeheartedly ... implying that others on TV her age should do so as well. 'The way you survive in television is by having plenty of tricks in your bag and not doing things for too long. There's a lot of moaning about women and ageism on television,' she told the *Daily Mail*. 'We could have a "Why aren't there more old, fat or ugly women on television?" argument if you like ... but why should there be?'

For her part, Mary insists she's never had to change the way she looks in order to progress. While the likes of Nigella Lawson have had plenty of media attention for how they look in front of the camera, Mary says she has never felt the pressure to dress differently while she's filming. 'I fuss about my hair, but otherwise I don't worry about what I look like,' she told the *Daily Mail*. 'I'm a bit scraggy around the neck and my husband always tells me I should wear a scarf, but I've no intention of doing anything about my wrinkles. I think cosmetic procedures are a waste of surgeons' time. I don't really have any aches and pains; I just feel terribly fortunate.' In another interview, with the Press Association, Mary added: 'Obviously I want to look good. You'll always see me blonde, I'll tell you that much, and I bother about my nails. The rest looks after itself.'

It wasn't just on the small screen that Mary started to forge a broadcasting career – she was soon snapped up for radio too. As technology developed, during the 1980s and 1990s, 'phone-ins' on radio shows became fashionable. The format was simple – the show would have an expert or a panel of experts in the studio to answer questions from the listeners. Alongside this, the appetite for TV cookery shows had filtered through into radio as well. Often cookery would be combined with a phone-in ... and this was the case on one show in particular.

Woman's Hour on BBC Radio 4 has become something of an institution on British radio. On air since just after the end of the Second World War, the magazine show covers all aspects of women's lives. An article celebrating the show's history in *The Journal* gives a comprehensive run-down of its most ground-breaking moments. It was first broadcast in 1946, bizarrely – it would seem – by a man. It was, wrote one of the show's presenters, Martha Kearney, 'scheduled at a time when morning chores and the lunchtime washing up would be finished and the children wouldn't be home from school'.

Among the show's early items was 'Cooking with whalemeat', which might seem strange now but was of interest because rationing was still widespread at the time, as well as features such as 'I married a lion tamer' and 'How to hang your husband's suit'.

On top of these were regular interviews with high-profile female celebrities – everyone from Eleanor Roosevelt in the 1940s to Winnie Mandela in the 1980s, before pulling off a huge coup with an exclusive with President Bill Clinton's former staffer Monica Lewinksy in the 1990s. Other female figures were put on a pedestal. The show mapped

Margaret Thatcher's ascent to leader of the Conservative Party and onwards to become prime minister. While her popularity wavered over the years, her role as a woman defining politics was a hot topic on the show that would run for years.

Ratings have remained consistently high, and Sue MacGregor CBE, who presented *Woman's Hour* from 1972 to 1987 before going on to host the morning news show *Today*, has said that she believes the programme's popularity stemmed from the early days when it was one of the first radio shows to cultivate an interactive relationship with its listeners. 'One of the first decisions the women listeners made was that they didn't want a man as the main presenter of their programme,' she told *The Journal*. 'Bizarrely, the first presenter was a middle-aged writer called Alan Ivieson who the listeners thought sounded patronising – they soon made their feelings apparent and he lasted just a few months.'

It seemed that one aim of *Woman's Hour* was to help women embrace being back in the home after the tumult of the Second World War. Some have said that the government wanted the BBC to put the show on as a way to encourage women to get back to what they were doing before the country came under attack and they had to get involved in the war effort by working in factories, making and flying aircraft, or working on the land in a way that they never had previously. So the show was a way of enticing women back to being homemakers.

The show hasn't changed greatly in format over the years, although some elements have been modernised. Fashion, for example, has been thrown into the modern mix – and sometimes quite risqué fashion, at that! Kearney noted: 'Jenni Murray chaired a heated debate on the thong, and I have been coached on how to walk on four-inch-high cerise marabou trimmed mules live on air.'

At times, the show has caused controversy, not least during its early days when the word 'vagina' was used during a feature about women's health. This caused outrage among some of the more sensitive members of the audience, and immediately the show's producers decided euphemisms should be used for particular terms from then on. For decades afterwards the term 'birth canal' was preferred, so worried were radio bosses that another storm would erupt.

The show's staple, however, was always cookery. Throughout all the years it has aired, this has remained a constant. And once again, that's where Mary came in. From 1994 to 2010, she was a regular contributor to the show. She was used predominantly for the phone-ins, but would later host segments on food as well as giving her own advice for succeeding in the kitchen. Just as the show became part of the listeners' daily routine, so too did Mary's appearances on it. Her words of wisdom became something that women could rely on, a friendly figure to whom they could turn on a regular basis, who could help them with even the most seemingly trivial problems they were encountering in the kitchen. No problem was too small or too big – Mary was always on hand to help. In particular, Mary's annual Christmas cookery phone-in became the stuff of legend, as she helped stressed housewives and homemakers navigate the maze that was the kitchen during the festive season. *Daily Telegraph* columnist Allison Pearson wrote about how she would barely get through December without Mary's help on

Woman's Hour. Writing in the paper, Pearson said: 'Mary will rescue my Yule log, which is looking a lot like a dead baby crocodile, whip up a trifle and make me a cup of tea. Unflappable, boundlessly kind, fresh as a cupcake at 76, the cook has recruited a new army of fans with her appearance on the *Great British Bake Off*. Aga shall not wither her, nor custom stale her Pear Crostini. Mary was the star of the best *Woman's Hour* I can remember in ages, just her in the studio with Jane Garvey, a Baby Belling and half a century of culinary wisdom. "Never stick anything up a goose's bottom," she cautioned. I wouldn't dream of it.'

Of course, the kitchen is a place that has seen great change over the years while *Woman's Hour* has been on air. This was something the show's producers often had to take into account. 'People are always astonished when I say that only about 60 per cent of the population had a shiny new fridge in their kitchen,' said Sue MacGregor. 'But we did quite a lot of cooking recipes with people like Delia Smith and Mary Berry and I can remember that, during the week, I was never allowed to say to put something in the fridge because lots of women couldn't afford a fridge in their homes back then. However, we had the Saturday omnibus edition for women who were out at work during the week, and we decided that we could mention fridges on that show because we thought that if they had been out at work all week they could probably afford to buy one.' This was something Mary understood too, and she would often tailor her advice so that people who didn't have the latest gadgets wouldn't feel alienated.

Following her success on *Woman's Hour*, other radio work was offered to Mary. She was a regular on another Radio 4 phone-in called *Tuesday Call*. Then between 1995 and 1998 she was a regular contributer on *The Debbie Thrower Programme* on BBC Radio 2. As a guest on the first Monday of every month, Mary once again took calls on the phone-in, while on other occasions she presented topical food items.

Mary's work in broadcasting transformed her profile from a cookery writer into a media personality. It was a turn of events she had probably never dreamed of when she first started writing recipes for *Housewife* magazine on a freelance basis. Hers was a style that would, at times, seem incongruous, considering how the landscape of cooking TV developed over the years, with cookery shows being given the reality-show treatment. Suddenly it became popular to centre cookery shows around a strong-willed and opinionated chef, who was demanding and had incredibly high standards. Rarely were the efforts of mere civilians good enough for these hard taskmasters and, at times, it seemed as though serving up a Michelin-starred meal may not even satisfy. While programmes such as these found a solid fan base, surely Mary's place as a TV celebrity would be in doubt as a result? In fact, quite the opposite turned out to be true. As suddenly, it seems, as they rose in popularity, this kind of rapid-fire, high-pressure show was superseded by something altogether more gentle. Stuart Heritage, writing in the *Guardian* about another competitive series, the *Great British Menu*, described this trend. He said: 'Once upon a time, shipping a load of professional chefs into a TV studio together would have been a recipe for shouting and diva tantrums and endless tiresome piddling contests. The friendliness of the contestants has been the secret to the show's success this year, and it's been a genuine breath of fresh air.' Heritage wondered whether host Marco Pierre White was adapting to the times, or mellowing as he approached middle age. 'Sporadic *MasterChef* professional kitchen mishaps aside, it seems as if the rude TV chef is dead. So long as this doesn't mean that Gordon Ramsay will return with a new show about how much he loves kittens and moonbeams, I'd say that was a good thing.' The public's appetite for the more volatile types of cookery show seemed to have waned.

It appeared that cookery TV had come full circle. That sense of friendship and closeness Mary had first cultivated with her viewers and listeners in the 1960s and 1970s was valued once again. While Mary had never fallen out of fashion and remained perennially popular, it suddenly appeared an especially good thing that she had stuck to her guns and remained herself. For her part, Mary insists she would never have wanted to get involved in a show where shouting matches occurred.

'The combative style of most TV competitions puts me right off,' she told the *Daily Mail*. 'I don't see any reason to shout or swear or be hyped up. I want to encourage the contestants to bake, and people at home to think that they can make it too. It's not just entertainment, it's a giant cookery lesson.' In later interviews she would expand on that theme when talking about the *Great British Bake Off*. Talking to the *Radio Times*, Mary said: 'Once viewers have seen people attempt something like a Battenberg cake and get into trouble then I come along and slowly and carefully show them how to make the perfect Battenberg, stopping when it might go wrong and encouraging them to have a go at home. I don't use ingredients that people aren't going to use again.

And I don't make things complicated.' Helping people to enjoy cooking and healthy food is of prime importance to Mary; she told Kirsty Young: 'I really hope that people are taking note of all the cooking that is going on on telly. I think a lot of the cooking is a bit theatrical, but I think there are plenty of programmes that show you exactly what to do. And I hope it tempts people to cook at home.' And it was to be the *Great British Bake Off* that would not only put those principles into practice, but would also make Mary a primetime TV star.

CHAPTER 8

LET THE BAKE OFF BEGIN!

In 2010 Mary was on the brink of becoming a true primetime TV star – even if she didn't yet know it. A new series called the *Great British Bake Off* was being developed and it was to be Mary who would be the face of it. That summer, an independent British TV company called Love Productions was looking for its next big hit. The production company, which was founded in 2005, had quickly developed a reputation as one of the premier companies of its kind in Britain. It's fair to say that it had a very specific niche, having become known for its gritty reality TV documentaries. These included *Underage and Having Sex*, which was centred around the statistic that one in three British youngsters will have sex before their sixteenth birthday, and *8 Boys And Wanting A Girl*, which visited the home of 43-year-old Wendy Bowen who, as the title of the show suggested, had given birth to eight sons but was desperate to conceive a daughter ... resulting in her 'biological clock ticking into an obsession'. TV during the 2000s has often been criticised for not being sufficiently imaginative and for appealing to the lowest common denominator – favouring scandal and formulaic programming over inspiring, well-crafted shows. But Love Productions didn't shy away from 'issues' and so was proving very successful in this climate; it had continued to bag sizeable ratings despite the fragmentation of audiences across multiple channels since the introduction of Freeview in the early 2000s. But by the late 2000s some of their tried-and-tested formats at last seemed to be faltering, and now Love Productions was looking for something different.

Cookery shows at the beginning of the millennium were as popular as they had always been – in fact, if anything, they were becoming more popular. It was time for Love Productions to move into this lucrative market. They wanted a competitive cookery show, but with a twist. At this time baking was back in fashion in Britain, thanks to a love for all things retro, and soon the biting recession would further encourage people to stay at home and have fun for free – or at least, very little outlay. Combining two elements – competitive cookery and baking – seemed like the perfect mix for a new TV show. And so the *Great British Bake Off* was born. The title was similar to the *Great British Menu*, another cookery competition which saw top British chefs compete for the chance to cook one course of a four-course banquet for the great and the good, including the Queen and the British Ambassador to France. When announcing the show in mid-2010, Love's managing director Richard McKerrow promised a 'warm and celebratory' series that would 'tell the history of Britain through baking'. He added: 'Baking is quintessentially British and it's the perfect feelgood subject for these rather straitened times. We want nothing less than to get the whole country baking again.'

And it didn't take long for the show to be commissioned by a major TV channel: BBC2 snapped it up. It was no surprise that this channel went for the *Great British Bake Off*, as it had long been the port of call for major cookery competition shows. It had been the birthplace of *MasterChef*, which had recently been relaunched, as well as the *Great British Menu*, and a host of other cookery shows from the likes of Nigella Lawson, Jamie Oliver and Delia Smith, as well as Mary herself.

Now that the TV show had a home, the producers had to go about finding their stars.

The other judge was to be Paul Hollywood. In some respects he and Mary couldn't be more different. But in other ways their lives – and their routes to the top of their profession – mirror each other in a rather uncanny way.

Born in 1966 in Wallasey, Merseyside, baking seemed to be in Paul's blood. His great-great-grandfather had been head baker at the Adelphi Hotel in Liverpool, while dad John owned a chain of bakeries, and one of his brothers has a successful wholesale baking business. As a child Paul was brought up above one of his father's bakeries. His first memory was making gingerbread biscuits with his mum, who was a graphic designer, and his dad at the age of five. Similar to Mary, Paul's teenage years were characterised by a relaxed attitude to academic work – not atypical for a lot of young people at that time. 'Dad was always in bed in the afternoons because of getting up in the early hours to bake,'

Paul told the *Daily Mail*. 'It's one of the reasons I didn't want to be a baker initially. I was a bed person; I think most teenagers are. But eventually you realise that getting up at dawn on a summer's morning is the best time. The roads are quiet, you can think, and you work while everyone else is sleeping.'

But back then, when it came to choosing what he wanted to do with his life, it seemed baking wasn't on the menu. So instead Paul decided to take a more artistic route and plumped for a course in sculpture at Wallasey School of Art. Paul, who had grown his hair to his shoulders, seemed to be following quite a hippyish path, as was fashionable among youngsters back then. Another similarity between him and Mary was that neither particularly enjoyed their studies, and instead of completing his course in sculpture, Paul quit to pursue a career in the food industry. He says his dad made him an offer he struggled to turn down. 'He said if I jacked it in and worked for him instead he'd give me £500, but only as long as I cut my hair,' Paul told the *Daily Mail*. 'That was a lot of cash in the mid-eighties. My mates would go clubbing and stop by the bakery in the early hours for something to eat. It upset me a bit to miss out on partying, but baking was what I wanted to do.'

Slowly, Paul started to work his way up the baking hierarchy, just as Mary had done from her early journalistic contributions right up to becoming an established author and broadcaster. At first he worked at one of his father's bakeries in Lincoln in the east of England. John Hollywood had a country-wide chain, and before long Paul was managing a handful of outlets. He later went on to be in charge of others back home on

Merseyside. By now he had firmly established a love of baking – it was not only a hobby, but his profession, and one that he was excelling at.

Bigger things were on the horizon, though. After working his way from the bottom up, Paul was soon noticed by established names in the hospitality world, and he had five-star hotels rushing to sign him up to work in their kitchens. It seemed that, after having taken a more relaxed approach to work during his teenage years, Paul had found his drive and ambition. Jobs as head baker at a number of prestigious hotels, including The Dorchester, the Chester Grosvenor and Spa and The Cliveden, followed. 'I was passionate and very competitive,' Paul told the *Daily Mail*. 'I wanted to become the best. Mix passion with a competitive streak and ambition and you've got a recipe to do whatever you want. Anyone who's successful will have one or all three of those traits.'

Soon hotels abroad heard about Paul's reputation as a master baker, and they came after him. Much like Mary, Paul was about to get used to being headhunted. His hard work had paid off and now his reputation preceded him. By now Paul was in his late twenties, and he was offered the chance to move to Cyprus. There was a job going at the plush Anassa hotel, and Paul brought his very British brand of baking to the Cypriot community as well as holidaymakers from around the world. High teas, scones and clotted cream were all on his menu. 'I flew out for an interview thinking it would just be a jolly for two days but came back really wanting to work there, which was so different to my normal character,' Paul told the *Daily Mail*. 'I'd always been such a home bird. When I moved to Cyprus, Mum gave it three weeks – I stayed for six years.' Not only was his time in

Cyprus a professional triumph, but it changed the course of his personal life, too. While working at the Anassa, Paul met fellow Brit Alexandra, who was working at the resort as a PADI diving instructor. Keen to soak up everything the island had to offer, Paul enlisted in classes and he and Alexandra fell in love, marrying a year later. They later had a son, Josh, before moving back to Britain and setting up home in the quiet Kent countryside.

As life in Cyprus was ticking along nicely, though, Paul happily stumbled across the chance to become a TV star. As if by fate, a camera crew arrived at the hotel where he worked to film a programme with respected food critic, Thane Prince. The producers needed someone from the hotel's kitchen to do a piece to camera. And that's where Paul came in. 'The crew asked me to do something to camera – I'd never done anything like that before,' Paul told the *Daily Mail*. 'The director said I should work in TV. I thought, "Yeah, right!" But when I came back to the UK two years later in 1999 I called him and within two months filmed a series with James Martin called *Use Your Loaf*.' James has remained a close friend and is godfather to Paul's son.

More TV work followed his big break and, like Mary, Paul became a regular on the daytime television circuit. Appearances on *The Generation Game*, *The Heaven and Earth Show*, ITV1's phenomenally successful *This Morning*, *Ready Steady Cook* and *The Alan Titchmarsh Show* all followed, as well as shows such as *Good Food Live* on the Good Food channel, while he has also been in demand as a guest speaker at several food festivals, including the Cumbrian Food Festival, and the BBC Good Food Show and the Cake and Bake Show, both in London. He has also become a published author, writing two books. *100 Great Breads* was released in 2004 and won him the Gourmand World Cookbook Award for Top Bread and Pastry Book in 2005 – the cookbook world's equivalent of taking home an Oscar. And following the success of the first two series of *GBBO*, Paul released *How to Bake* in 2012.

But while the TV and media work made Paul a household name, he never forgot his roots in baking. He has since set up his own artisan bread-baking company, which he manages to this day. It supplies delis and restaurants around London and the South East. One of his products attracted many column inches in 2008, after he created an almond and Roquefort sourdough recipe. If it sounds expensive, that's because it is. At the time, newspapers said it was the most expensive bread to be made in Britain, with Paul describing it in interviews as the 'Rolls-Royce of loaves'. The plush London department store Harrods sold it for an eye-watering £15 a loaf. Explaining the hefty price tag, Paul said that the Roquefort came from a specialist cheese supplier in France and cost £15 a kilo. The flour for the bread, meanwhile, was handmade by a specialist miller in Wiltshire.

If there was anyone who would know a thing or two about baking, it seemed it would be Paul. And so when the *GBBO* producers came to deciding who would be the perfect fit for the role of the tough-talking judge, Paul came to mind. Sue Perkins, who was later picked to co-present the show, was already in talks with the producers. She knew Paul after having been involved in a string of food programmes, and they had met on a number of occasions. She suggested him as a good choice to sit alongside Mary. To the producers, he seemed like the perfect down-to-earth character. He had said in one interview with the *Daily Mail*: 'All I want to do is bake. Whether I do that on TV or on the moon, I'm still just a baker.' Paul's straight-talking manner would balance out Mary's poise and perfect manners. Paul explained in an interview how it all came about. 'I was approached by Sue Perkins to take part, as she had seen some of my stuff on the Good Food channel,' Paul told his local newspaper, the *Kent Messenger*. 'The BBC then rang me to talk me through the idea and introduce me to fellow judge, baking writer Mary Berry. Then, at the start of April, we began filming around the country for the six-part series.'

With the judging panel sorted, all the producers now needed before they launched the show to great fanfare was a presenter, or presenters. Sue Perkins was already being looked at as a possibility. Born in 1969 in East Dulwich, London, Sue was educated at the independent Croham Hurst School for Girls in Croydon before later winning a place to read English at New Hall at the University of Cambridge, graduating in 1990. It was while she was studying at Cambridge that Sue got her first taste of success as an entertainer. She was a member of Footlights, the amateur dramatics club with a prestigious reputation, responsible for launching the careers of stars such as Robert Webb, Sandi Toksvig, Gryff Rhys Jones and Eric Idle, to name but a few, who had all been members while at the university. Sue later became president of Footlights, and it was there that she met fellow student and actress Mel Giedroyc. Mel was born in 1968 in Epsom, Surrey; her father was a history writer of Polish-Lithuanian descent who had come to England in 1947. Perhaps due to her mixed heritage, Mel showed an aptitude for learning and speaking foreign languages, and after studying at Oxford High School for Girls, she too won a place at Cambridge to read Italian language and literature at New Hall. After performing together at Footlights, including at various festivals, and having established a solid friendship, the pair decided to try and make a go of being a duo once they graduated. After gigging at stand-up comedy events, they eventually got their breakthrough. They were picked to write material for the television series *French and Saunders*, the sketch show starring another female comedy duo, Dawn French and Jennifer Saunders. Mel and Sue would later go on to be compared to them as their partnership flourished. But the pair really started to make waves on TV with the launch of their own show. And as with both Mary and Paul, it was on daytime TV. Together they launched the popular Channel 4 show *Light Lunch*. The format was simple – and as the title suggested, it revolved around food. Celebrity chefs had to cook lunch for the duo's celebrity guests. Unlike Mary and Paul, Mel and Sue did none of the cooking, but their irreverent, humorous style made the show a big hit. It was later moved to an early evening spot and renamed *Late Lunch*. To add to the banter, the studio audience were expected to bring in their own 'lunch' to eat during the show, and were each given £3 to cover the cost of this. They were encouraged to bring in unusual food, their own creations, or food that in some way related to that day's celebrity guest – and the most creative ideas would be shown on camera. The series ran for two years, and soon TV producers were fighting to sign up Mel and Sue – as they had become known – for their next venture. In 1999, Channel 4's rival network, ITV, signed them to front a new comedy panel show called *Casting*

Couch. This was a great opportunity for the girls and exposed them to a wider, more adult audience, as the programme aired in a late evening slot. Unfortunately, though, the ratings did not meet expectations and the ITV bosses chose not to re-commission it after its first series. Other side projects included returning to where it all started, appearing together again in a Dawn French and Jennifer Saunders *Mamma Mia!* sketch for Comic Relief in March 2009, as well as performing together on various radio programmes, with them proving especially popular on BBC Radio 4.

After a while, the duo decided they wanted to explore solo projects. While their friendship remained as solid as ever, they both wanted to try out new things. While Sue has since tried her hand at a range of different ventures, including a stint on *Celebrity Big Brother* and presenting on the now-defunct Channel 4 breakfast show *RI:SE*, she quickly found a niche presenting food shows. In April 2007, she took part in *Edwardian Supersize Me* for the BBC with food critic Giles Coren. The pair spent a week eating the equivalent of a wealthy Edwardian couple's diet, while dressing in traditional clothes from the era. They decided it was a winning formula and the duo returned in May 2008 with a series called *The Supersizers Go ...* The concept involved them spending a week eating food based on certain diets. The first instalment saw them survive for a week on Second World War rations. In the second episode, they moved back in time to the English Restoration period, followed by the Victorian era, the 1970s and the Elizabethan and Regency periods. Sue also appeared on *Celebrity MasterChef* in 2006.

Meanwhile, Mel worked on a range of programmes

including co-presenting a daytime chat show and starring in a BBC sitcom. She also appeared in three series of the twice BAFTA-nominated cult sketch show *Sorry I've Got No Head*, as well as the West End musical *Eurobeat* and the popular teen drama, *Sadie J*.

But after working separately for four years, the opportunity arose to work together again. The producers behind the *Great British Bake Off* had already been talking to Sue about the possibility of her fronting the show and considering whom she could be paired with. Keen to make sure that a show about baking didn't become too serious or staid, they wanted to make sure whoever presented it would keep things light and fluffy. It seemed like an obvious decision to reunite Mel and Sue. Sue first hinted at their reunion when she appeared on *Friday Night with Jonathan Ross*, saying that they would be working on something together in 2010. Although both were up for the challenge, Sue admitted in an interview with TV industry magazine *Broadcast* that she found the prospect daunting, adding: 'We'd both changed hugely as individuals.' Speaking ahead of the first series, Sue added that she wasn't sure whether they would work together full-time, but that they were excited about the *Great British Bake Off*. 'We're keen to keep our new identities but the door's definitely open,' she said.

So, with the judges and presenters in place, the filming was due to start over the summer months of 2010. For the first series, it was decided that the show would tour the UK, with each episode taking in a new location that had a particular link to the world of British baking. But before filming even got off the ground, potential problems arose that threatened to jeopardise the whole thing. One location the producers were keen to visit was Bourton-on-the-Water, in Gloucestershire. Set in the heart of the picturesque Cotswolds, the small village was its own slice of baking history, famed for its afternoon teas, scones and clotted cream. It would be the perfect place to film an episode, Love Productions felt. And Mary was keen to see what the bakers from that part of the country could cook up for her and Paul, later saying: 'I love the South West, and my favourite episode of *Bake Off* was definitely Mousehole.'

However, some Bourton locals were less than keen to see *Bake Off* pitch up in the town. The local newspaper, the *Gloucestershire Echo*, reported prominently in its pages: 'Plans to film a new television series at Bourton-on-the-Water have cooked up a storm.' The producers had planned to take over the village green, the report continued. On it they planned to set up a large marquee in which the filming would take place. But the parish council was up in arms at the plans. They said that their 'cherished centrepiece' would be 'overwhelmed' by the arrival of so many people, which would include a huge entourage of vehicles. Parish and district councillor Sheila Jeffery said: 'They are trying to cash in because Bourton is known. We're too small and too precious to have them trample all over us. It's a massive amount to put in the village centre.' Mrs Jeffery also questioned whether the BBC had thought through their reasoning for wanting to film in Bourton-on-the-Water in the first place: 'And why do they want to come here? We're not known for cakes; the Cotswolds is known for its wolds and sheep.' According to the parish council's minutes, Love Productions proposed to set up a 18m by 12m marquee on the green sward, a gazebo to store equipment, a generator on an 8m truck and also to bring some 15 other support vehicles. It would, the parish council claimed, destroy the quaint atmosphere of the local area by causing an influx of extra visitors and creating chaos, unless the filming was properly monitored and controlled. Councillor Tim Faulkner was one of the parish councillor who objected strongly. He said: 'TV companies can be an absolute nightmare – they never do what they say they're going to do.' Colleagues also wondered if the green was even wide enough to accommodate the ambitious marquee, in which Mary and Paul would judge the would-be bakers' results. Councillor Alan Palmer was particularly worried about this point, asking: 'Have they taken account of the trees?' The council was also concerned that the BBC hadn't made it clear whether or not they would pay for using the green. Parish council village green bookings committee chairman Gill Crippen said: 'We only want to give permission if the marquee's an acceptable size and lorries, equipment and other paraphernalia are not parked on the green or alongside it. If they abide by this, I think people will genuinely welcome something of this order in the village and it will enhance it. We should point out we have some anxieties and have an on-site meeting.' There was one person, however, who agreed with the move to bring the *Great British Bake Off* to the area. Chairman Bryan Sumner said: 'I feel the programme's sufficiently relevant and good for Bourton if it doesn't overwhelm us.' After the meeting, parish clerk Sue Cretney said: 'It's a one-off series going around the country, with each programme showcasing baking of that area. They thought of the Cotswolds because we're synonymous with tea rooms.'

This was not the first time film crews were not welcomed with open arms to the Cotswolds. In 2006 Stow Town Council had snubbed movie-makers, fearing they would disrupt trade. They regretted it after discovering that the filming they'd blocked was for former Brockworth schoolboy Simon Pegg's film *Hot Fuzz*, which went on to become a blockbuster. Nevertheless, the BBC didn't want to cause upset. They understood that there was sufficient concern about filming the *Great British Bake Off* in Bourton-on-the-Water for it to be problematic, and withdrew. But while this may have been the first controversy in the programme's history, it would by no means be the last.

With that hurdle left behind, filming got into full swing. More than 1,000 hopefuls entered the audition process, before being whittled down to 10 finalists. But getting to that stage was no mean feat in itself. 'Every person who makes it into the marquee has passed a rigorous series of tests,' Anna Beattie, the executive producer and creator of the *Great British Bake Off* concept, said in an interview with the *Daily Telegraph*. Anna had come up with the idea for the show after talking to a friend who had seen 'bake-offs' in America, where they are hugely popular. The *GBBO* contestants all filled out long application forms and, if they met all the requirements, this allowed them through to the next stage. They were then quizzed by one of the show's researchers in a 45-minute telephone interview. The next stage saw successful contestants invited to London, where they were asked to bring two of their most successful 'bakes', to see if their culinary skills were really up to scratch. Following that was a screen test and a further interview with a senior producer. All that might seem enough, but think again. If the would-be baking superstars succeeded at all those tests, they then had to go through to a second audition, baking two recipes for Mary and Paul, this time in front of rolling cameras, to see how they would interact with the two judges and how they would come across on screen. The final hurdle that all contestants had to pass was a forensic interview with one of the show's psychologists. The producers have a duty of care to all contestants and they needed to make sure they would be able to cope with the stresses, strains and overall pressure of filming for up to 16 hours a day, potentially for weeks on end. It's no wonder contestants on reality shows are often told they're 'all winners' for even getting on to the show in the first place.

Finally, after the lengthy audition process, Mary and Paul had their 10 contestants. They were Welsh bus driver Mark Withers, Scottish freelance food writer Lea Harris, Marks & Spencer commercial manager Miranda Gore Browne, Solihull housewife Jasminder Randhawa, David Chambers from Milton Keynes, Annetha Mills, Manchester police sergeant Louise Brimelow, shop owner Jonathan Shepherd, fourth-generation baker Ruth Clemens and debt collector Edd Kimber. Over the course of six episodes, they would battle it out, with Mary and Paul eventually finding a single winner. After the controversy surrounding Bourton, filming had moved elsewhere in the Cotswolds for the first episode. Later filming continued at Sandwich and Sarre Mill, in Thanet, Kent, with the aim of enabling the contestants to find out about a place where traditional bread-baking skills are still used. They would later cook puddings in Bakewell, pasties in Cornwall and scones at Scone Palace, in Perthshire, Scotland. The travelling alone seemed exhausting enough, but with filming now getting going, the set of the show was a hive of activity too. Both Mel and Sue kept the atmosphere jovial and lively with their witty asides and comic interludes, whether the cameras were rolling or switched off. In particular, they became adept at teasing Paul, gently poking fun at his hairstyle and patting him affectionately as they prepared to film their segments. Meanwhile, food producers were constantly on standby between takes. While the contestants were by and large left to their own devices, the food producers helped any who were in particularly sticky situations, giving tips on a recipe or providing new ingredients. 'We help the bakers to a certain degree,' Faenia Moore, the programme's home economist, told the *Daily Telegraph* in an interview. 'We do show the disasters, but you don't want to set anyone up for a fall.'

The first contestants to be thrown off the show were Mark and Lea, at the end of the first episode. After her exit from the show, Lea told the *Scotsman*: 'Let's just say cakes are very temperamental and every one of the cakes looked completely different from the other ... There were some tears, but when you're on camera and cooking to a time limit it is quite stressful. It's just off camera, but I managed to drop my signature bake – pistachio and cranberry cake – on the floor. And I almost set my clothes on fire, which you can't see on TV. With five minutes to spare, I managed to stick the five bits of my cake back together.'

Mary has spoken of how impressive many of the contestants have been – despite their tears – given that it is a competition among amateurs: 'I feel sorry for them,' she told *Stella* magazine. 'The emotion comes because they are cross with themselves. They think they can do it, then something goes wrong. But the lovely thing is the family atmosphere and the kindness; contestants lend each other ingredients, they offer each other space in their ovens.' The producers don't proactively seek out or have a hand in the crises sometimes caught on camera – the drama comes down to the fact that we're watching normal people trying their best in a very high-pressure environment. Mary said on *Desert Island Discs*, 'Well, they are all amateur bakers. Everything you see is absolutely genuine. No dramas, and you know, there isn't a camera going, ah she's crying, shall we put that in? They are very likely not to put it in. If people do things that don't work and a sauce doesn't set or something, the camera is on it, and then later on either Paul Hollywood or I will say, to avoid that we do such and such. So people really get the feel, it is a baking lesson in disguise.'

But as the contestants continued to battle it out in that first series, it was the chemistry between Mary and Paul that most impressed the producers. They seemed to be a match made in heaven. Despite the age gap there seemed to be an instant connection. Mary regularly voiced her respect for Paul in pre-series interviews. Paul, for his part, seemed to be the only one who could get away with calling Mary by the nickname 'Bezza'. No one had known quite how well things would go until the filming started. And as each episode was filmed, they appeared to settle in to a 'good cop, bad cop' routine – with Mary decidedly playing the good cop. Meanwhile, Paul was the 'antidote' – the harsher judge as often seen on other reality TV programmes, cultivating a firm-but-fair on-screen persona. He only judged the finished product, and never minced his words. Meanwhile, Mary was always measured in her criticism. The worst you would hear from her would be: 'I'm really disappointed,' or 'I don't like this at all.' 'It's not about being beastly – we're not a bit like *MasterChef*,' she has said.

Journalist Sarah Stephens from the *Daily Telegraph* was invited on to the set. She scrutinised the judging process, and wrote: 'The judging itself is fascinating to watch. During a technical bake (the round in which contestants have no prior knowledge of the recipes), the finished products are lined up on a table anonymously, while the bakers themselves sit on stools facing away from the bakes. It looks contrived, but it ensures no one can influence the judges. Meanwhile Berry and Hollywood make their way along the table, commenting and tasting as they go. "This is over-baked," Hollywood complains. "Structure's all wrong." "Pastry's lovely on this one," Berry says, breaking through with her fork. Decisions are swift and definite.'

But for all that Mary and Paul's on-screen chemistry would cement the show's reputation, Mary admits that they don't always see eye to eye. For one, Mary has refused to be combative towards the contestants. 'I wouldn't have taken part if I had been expected to make nasty comments,' she told the *Daily Mail*. She and Paul would often have to spend hours deliberating over who was to stay and who was to go. On one occasion, it took them five hours to work out who would be cut from the show prior to a semi-final in the first series. Their personal approaches to baking meant that they often clashed.

'Mary's angle is home baking; mine is professional, so we meet in the middle but with all the same passion and drive,' Paul said in an interview with the *Daily Mail*. Although he admitted he'd learnt a lot from her – specifically to use Stork margarine, which she had come to know after working for the brand all those years ago at PR firm Bensons. 'I always used butter in my cakes before, but Mary said I should use a mixture of butter and Stork – you get the flavour from butter but the Stork sustains the crumb, making it lighter,' Paul told the *Daily Mail*.

Mary herself has been quite forthright about the differences between her and Paul's approaches to the judging process. 'Paul makes brilliant bread, and I've learnt from him, but I don't agree with him on lots of things,' Mary said in one interview. 'Paul takes a more professional line: every biscuit must be identical. It's not like that in real life; we're amateur bakers, and if there's one that's a bit of a wobbly shape or overcooked – not all ovens cook evenly – well, Mum has that one.'

She added: 'When I was asked to be a judge, I said I wanted to be myself. I didn't want to shout like some other television judges. I also said I was a very bad bread maker, so would the programme makers find someone to help on the bread scene? I admire my fellow judge Paul Hollywood enormously, though we often argue. He believes presentation and uniformity are paramount; I'm more interested in taste. I don't mind if one bun is smaller than the others, or if there's a little pastry cracking, though I don't want a soggy bottom.'

And that was perhaps the only thing, it seemed, that could rile Mary – a soggy bottom. While her criticism was always measured, a soggy base to the pastry quickly became the sure-fire way to get Mary's goat. This would be a phrase that Mary would return to, time and time again, as subsequent series of *GBBO* returned to the screens. Even in interviews she would repeat it. The soggy bottom was once even described by the *Guardian* as Mary's 'nemesis', while Mary called it her catchphrase. Meanwhile, her loyal fans would often discuss the perils of a soggy bottom. It was, as far as Mary was concerned, the ultimate faux pas – the way to immediately set yourself up for possible elimination from the show. The phrase seemed to have such a cult following that Kirsty Young pressed Mary quite hard on it when she appeared on *Desert Island Discs*. Asked whether soggy bottoms were the 'greatest sin' in the kitchen, Mary replied: 'Soggy bottoms are ... if there is one thing I really don't like in a quiche. And you can imagine, when I go to charity lunches and things, [the committee always] make things like quiches. And you lift it up and it is just underbaked and it is horrible to eat, but I can never just tuck it under a lettuce leaf, because somebody is going to be hurt when they clear the plates.' On the topic of how to avoid the soggy bottom, Mary added: 'A soggy bottom you avoid by baking blind, and then I always put it in on a hot baking sheet, nice thin pastry underneath, dry it out, then put the filling in.'

Soggy bottoms and the occasional tussle with Paul aside, Mary quickly adapted to filming and enjoyed the process immensely as the first series progressed. 'The atmosphere is lovely. If people are in a panic, Mel and Sue will help them,' she said in an interview with the *Daily Mail*. 'And the contestants support each other, which is delightful.'

The other stars of the show agreed. Speaking to the *Daily Mail*, Paul described the atmosphere on set as 'lovely and completely genuine', adding that Mel and Sue are like his 'naughty sisters'. He added: 'They're always pulling faces, or winding me up and I have to say, "Hey, you two, shush!" We have some real giggles ... A couple of times I've rolled out of that tent in tears from laughing so much.' And Sue admitted she loved her new role, not least, she joked, because it wasn't one of her most demanding. 'We just have to pop up and ask "what's the crumb density on that focaccia?"' she told *Broadcast*. On a more serious note, Sue said that she could tell the series was destined to be a success. 'It's open and it's warm,' she told *Broadcast*. 'There's no censure and they're all real characters, not screeching TV presenter wannabes. These people want to do things well; they tell us they like baking because it gives them two hours to do nothing else but focus on the task at hand. And ultimately, our job is making sure ten people are happy doing it.'

Despite the cosy on-set atmosphere, Mary quickly realised that there were pitfalls involved in judging a baking competition: specifically, the fact that you had to taste so much cake, repeatedly and over a sustained period of time. Mary had always held health, fitness and well-being in high regard. Indeed, over the course of three series of the *Great British Bake Off*, putting on weight is not something Mary's risked. As early as the first series Mary said she developed a technique to keep herself from piling on the pounds. 'I love cake, but I have no wish to be large and for people to say, "I don't want to get like her; she's the one who makes the cakes,"' she told the *Daily Mail*. 'Doing *Bake Off*, I have to taste a fair-sized piece of each cake, which can mean 36 slices a day. So when I'm filming, all I have for lunch is soup, and I'm very careful the next day.'

Finally, after months of filming, the series had its transmission date scheduled – 17 August 2010. Despite all the hype and preparation, no one knew whether or not the *Great British Bake Off* would be a success. However, the good news was that it did prove to be a hit – both in the ratings figures and with the critics. The first episode attracted a very respectable 2.24 million viewers. And, after rave reviews from critics, viewing figures shot up to a very impressive 3 million for the second episode, which was then sustained for the rest of the series. The controllers at BBC2 and the producers behind the show couldn't have been more delighted.

The reviews were overwhelmingly positive as well. In particular, they focused on Mary's on-screen relationship with Paul. Despite their ups and downs, they made a formidable duo. The *Guardian* described their double act as the 'secret weapon' of the show, going as far as to say that it was potentially one of the best judging combinations to have appeared on a reality TV show. And others agreed. The *Leicester Mercury* declared: 'Think *MasterChef* but with bread and cakes. With the competition being judged by Mary Berry, the undisputed Queen of Cakes, and Paul Hollywood, one of Britain's leading artisan bakers, the ten contestants have a lot to prove as they push their baking skills to the limit.' The series prompted debate about the relative merits of different approaches to baking. Later in the series, Anne Harrison, from the Women's Institute, wrote in the *Guardian*: 'The judges on the *Great British Bake Off* have very different styles. Mary Berry is someone even I would be nervous to cook for. The other judge, Paul Hollywood, has obviously spent his life in commercial baking. I don't always agree with him. To test a scone, the WI teaches that you don't need to cut it with a knife – you should be able to pull it apart along its natural split. Hollywood said that was wrong – but if you cut a scone with a knife, it compacts the texture as you press down. It's the same with gingerbread.'

For her part, Mary was delighted with the response to the show. Not only had her career as a TV star been rejuvenated, but more importantly to her, baking was once again being talked about.

'I've been "rediscovered" at the age of 76,' she told the *Daily Mail*. 'I'm joyfully surprised by how successful the *Great British Bake Off* has been. I think people enjoy it because it's entirely genuine. Paul and I decide who stays and who goes. The producers would probably like a chap in the final and people from different regions, but it's never mentioned.'

If that was the case, it was a happy coincidence that right up to the final of series one, men and women from all over Great Britain were represented. Eventually Edd Kimber, a 26-year-old debt collector who worked for a Yorkshire bank, was crowned the greatest amateur baker in Britain. An unlikely star baker, you might think, but he succeeded at every stage of the competition. His bakes, Mary and Paul agreed in unison, were the best by far. Neither could fault him. But Edd had double the reason to be delighted with his win – it meant he could give up his day job, which he loathed. 'It was the worst job ever – I absolutely hated it,' Edd said in an interview with the *Daily Telegraph* some months after his win. 'People would swear at me hourly and they'd send you round to people's houses in pairs in case things turned nasty. I used to spend most of my time looking up recipes online; I'm surprised they didn't fire me.' Perhaps the real power of the *Great British Bake Off* was proven by the fact that within 12 months Edd was no longer a debt collector but instead had a recipe book in the shops, was running a series of cookery classes and was even appearing on food roadshows up and down the country. He had launched his own brand of baked produce too, simply called The Boy Who Bakes. Explaining the thought process behind the name, Edd told the *Daily Telegraph* with a laugh: 'Well, I am a boy and I do bake. I wanted to make it clear that anyone can bake. In the past it's been associated with housewives and the Women's Institute; but these days you get bakers from all walks of life.'

And that, it seemed, was the beauty of *GBBO*. Finally, baking didn't appear to be something reserved for housewives in the kitchen. It was cool, trendy; something that even young men could enjoy. After ticking all the boxes – ratings, great reviews and cultural impact – it was no surprise that BBC2 was quick to snap up a second series of *Bake Off* for 2011.

Viewers couldn't wait to see Mary and Paul back on their screens. The demand was so high that BBC2 also commissioned a one-off documentary called *The Great British Wedding Cake*. This aired on 20 April 2011, and saw Mary and Paul explore the history of wedding cakes around the country. They charted the history of the wedding cake, from its earliest incarnation as the Tudor bride cake that weighed a ton and was baked wrapped in pastry. They also revealed the story that is said to have led to the creation of the classic tiered wedding cake – a baker who spied a London church from his window fashioned his wedding cake in its image. On top of that, Mary and Paul recounted stories about how Queen Victoria introduced the world to royal icing, and revealed that it was the rise in second marriages which led to the huge range of different wedding cakes available today. Interspersed throughout the documentary, Mary and Paul were reunited with the three finalists from the first series of *Bake Off* to set them a one-off challenge to bake a wedding cake. The ratings were moderate at 1.6 million, but served to build excitement and anticipation for the second series of the *Great British Bake Off*, which was just around the corner. And while the first outing had been an unrivalled success, the show was about to get even bigger.

CHAPTER 9

THE BAKE OFF CONTINUES

It came as no surprise that the *Great British Bake Off* was to be re-commissioned and would return to TV screens across Britain the following year, alongside a raft of other cookery programmes. After the success of the first series, it seemed like an obvious, natural progression for the show – and, of course, for Mary. The combination of Mary with Paul, Mel and Sue was a vital ingredient in making the first series such a storming success. They were all invited back for the show's second outing and preparations for filming soon got under way.

The show's producers were keen to capitalise on the popularity of the first series and make the second outing even bigger and better than before. The first change they made was the number of contestants. It was decided to increase the number of people competing from 10 to 12. The long audition process kicked off, and eventually an eclectic group of would-be master bakers was selected, after just as much deliberation as before. They included Janet Basu, Yasmin Limbert, Mary-Anne Boermans, Holly Bell, Joanne Wheatley, Keith Batsford, Simon Blackwell, Robert Billington, Jason White, Urvashi Roe, Ben Frazer and Ian Vallance.

On top of that, the series consisted of 10 episodes, rather than six. The four extra episodes were in response to the public's obvious appetite for the show. The first series had been an unknown quantity – when the BBC commissioned it, they'd had high hopes, but didn't know how it would fare with viewers. But after overwhelming support from fans of the show as well as critics, it seemed natural to order more episodes. The new series was starting to take shape.

The final ingredient in the pre-production process that the producers had to work out was where they were going to film the second series. Having spent the first series travelling the country's baking hot spots, had the novelty worn off? They couldn't do the same thing again for the show's second outing, surely? What's more, constantly moving filming around the country was fine if there were only six episodes, but could become tiring and expensive when there were an extra four to film. So it was decided that, rather than turning *GBBO* into a roadshow, the whole series would be filmed in one location. After toying with various possible settings, the producers decided on Valentines Mansion, a large seventeenth-century house in Valentines Park, in Redbridge, London. The Grade II listed building was built in 1696 for Lady Tillotson, the widow of the Archbishop of Canterbury, but centuries later underwent extensive refurbishment financed by the Heritage Lottery Fund and the London Borough of Redbridge Council. The beautiful house, steeped in its rich history, would provide a quintessentially British backdrop for *GBBO*, and it was here that the TV crews behind the show prepared for what would prove to be another hugely successful series in the early summer of 2011.

And, as the series started to air in August that year, it seemed to be even more popular than the first. The viewing figures soared. The first episode attracted more than 3.1 million, rising steadily to a peak of just over 5 million in episode eight. These were better figures than anyone could have hoped for. And the critics seemed to think they knew the reason for the show's following – Mary. Even more effusively than before, they gushed about her on-screen chemistry with Paul, while newspapers and magazines across the country rushed to book interviews with her. No longer was Mary merely a cookery writer and occasional presenter of TV cookery shows. She was a star.

Of course Mary, with her usual modesty, continued to shrug off her new-found fame. It was, she said, just part of her mission statement to bring baking to the masses. And she was certainly succeeding.

But while Mary's popularity off screen grew, on screen the drama as *GBBO* neared its climax was reaching fever pitch. As more and more people tuned in to witness what culinary delights would be conjured up week after week, the competition became increasingly intense. After Janet Basu unexpectedly crashed out of the competition, three women remained – Jo Wheatley, Mary-Anne Boermans and Holly Bell. They were all popular, both with viewers and critics. Writing in the *Mail on Sunday*, Tom Parker-Bowles noted this, as well as the way in which baking had given rise to a level of drama that simply could not be scripted. He wrote:

'The final three contestants are eminently likeable, and talented too. There's Joanne, the pretty housewife who longs for a career. And Holly, precise and methodical, a perfectionist to the very marrow. And Mary-Anne, a culinary bibliophile who veers towards the experimental. All are modest and, in a thoroughly self-effacing way, desperate to win. TV chefs may shout, curse and hurl pans. TV bakers, on this evidence, are the epitome of good manners. Maternal is very much the new macho. But that is not to say that the contestants aren't, at times, overwhelmed by their emotions. There may not be tantrums, but there were plenty of tears as the weeks wore on. This is because baking itself is temperamental. It is a matter of science rather than art. Unlike a stew, where exact measurements are unnecessary, if you put the wrong amount of yeast in your bread, disaster follows. I have always been rather afraid of baking. I may be utterly confident about throwing together a pasta sauce, grilling a fish or roasting a joint, but ask me to make puff pastry and I will run for the hills. But, right now, baking is very much back in vogue.'

But while all three contestants were likeable, it was Jo who would triumph when the final was screened on 13 October. Aged 41 at the time of filming, she was affectionately described as the 'youngest grandmother in the competition'. From Essex originally, she had rediscovered her love of baking thanks to her nan. 'My nan has always been my inspiration for baking,' said Jo in an interview with the *Brentwood Gazette*. 'She would always make pastry and is a really good baker. I would go over to hers most weekends – she would make tarts and give me the offcuts of the pastry to make jam tarts. I've always baked, ever since then.' Jo had married her husband Richard at the age of 17, and settled down to have three boys, Billy, Jesse and Dylan. Rather than pursuing a career, she had dedicated her life to being a full-time mother and housewife, and a big part of this was her love of baking. She was totally self-taught through cookbooks and by watching TV shows like Mary's, and often baked up to 10 times a week for her family. On the show, Jo had explained how her children would give her marks out of 10 for their meals ... but would find it particularly funny to give her low scores. In Jo's typically down-to-earth manner, which made her a hit with viewers, she said: 'It makes me feel like putting their heads in the dinner.' Jo had also experienced tough times in her life. Her husband had got involved in crime and was sentenced to seven years in prison for his part in a money-laundering racket – something the tabloid press would later seize on after Jo became popular on *Bake Off*. In her typically dignified manner, Jo kept going, and after 25 years of dedicating her life to her family, Jo's sons and friends had encouraged her to apply for the show. 'I just entered on a whim, I didn't think too much about it ... I googled it and got the application form,' she told the *Brentwood Gazette*. 'I did wonder about entering or not, but I clicked the "yes" button in the end.' The show's producers loved her back story and, despite her nervousness, she went down a storm with Mary and Paul at her final auditions. She was selected for the competition and it was her time to shine.

Described in the press as 'sweet-faced and preternaturally girly', her bakes were almost always near-perfect throughout the series. That's not to say she didn't make mistakes and, at times, even seemed to come close to letting the pressure of the show get to her. This was particularly apparent on one occasion. During week six of the competition, and moments before Mary and Paul were due to start the judging process, Jo hit disaster. She had made a tower of cream-stuffed profiteroles as well as a limoncello and white chocolate *croquembouche*, the classic French choux pastry dessert. But suddenly, seemingly out of nowhere, it had collapsed. It couldn't be salvaged. But Mary concluded that the bake's 'outstanding deliciousness' would allow Jo to survive. Perhaps Mary, a mum herself, recognised something familiar in Jo's ambition and determination. It wasn't the only near-miss that Jo had, though. Another week, when Jo took on the task of making brandy snaps from Mary's own recipe, she encountered more problems. All seemed to be going fine as she placed the mixture in the oven to bake. The only snag was that she hadn't realised that the oven had been set to the 'defrost' function, meaning the snaps didn't rise. But once again, despite the blunder, Jo's talent shone through and she was saved. 'It was funny – in the final I baked like I do at home,' Jo told the *Brentwood Gazette*. 'I think I felt that by then I'd done the whole thing and experienced every bit of it. So on the final day, I didn't put the pressure on myself, I just enjoyed it. I didn't mind whether I came first, second or third, I really was just happy to have got that far. I didn't think I'd won. I heard them call out my name but I thought maybe they were doing it in reverse order. I looked up and saw my kids jumping up and down and my friends all cheering, and then I realised. It was an amazing feeling.'

Most of all, Jo said the best thing about the whole experience was Mary. For years she had followed Mary's work, admiring not only her recipes, which she regularly cooked at home, but also her incredible career path. As such, it was a huge honour when Mary complimented Jo after she cooked her own signature dish ... the Victoria Sponge. 'My greatest moment was when Mary said my Victoria sandwich was one of the best she'd ever tasted,' Jo said in an interview with the *Essex Chronicle*. 'It was a massive compliment coming from the lady I so respect.' And when asked in the same interview which cooks had influenced her over the years, Jo quickly responded: 'Mary, of course!' The feeling of respect was mutual. After triumphing in the competition, Mary spoke openly about how proud she was of Jo. In particular, Mary said she was delighted to see how Jo had grown as a person over the course of the series. No longer was she the shy, retiring housewife whose life was dedicated to bringing up her family. 'Jo was absolutely the right winner,' Mary said in an interview with the *Daily Mail*. 'And it was lovely to see how she came out of herself and grew much more confident.'

And with that boosted confidence came new opportunities for Jo. Like Mary, Jo also had a passion for the trusty storage-heating oven, the Aga. To begin with, she set up a blog called Jo's Blue Aga, dedicated to giving advice, tips and recipes to other Aga lovers. Following on from that, she secured the chance to hold a series of workshops in cupcake decorating, as well as Christmas hamper baking. Places were snapped up by her fans and the classes quickly became fully booked. But that was just the beginning of Jo's blossoming career as a celebrity baker. It seemed that her own life would start to mirror Mary's in more ways than one as she became increasingly high profile. Having noticed all the attention directed her way, at this point a publishing house approached

Jo to write her own book. She jumped at the chance and, in 2012, she released *A Passion For Baking*. During its first week of release it flew up the *Sunday Times* best-sellers list to number two in the non-fiction charts. Suddenly Jo was giving Mary a run for her money! 'I never dreamt I'd be able to write a book,' Jo told the *Brentwood Gazette*. 'It's easy to follow, with not too many ingredients and some really good flavours. That's how I wanted the book to be, very down to earth and practical. It covers all aspects of baking. I thought about what I would want to do if I did a cookery book and this is it.'

The aim of the book was to appeal to as broad a cross section of bakers as possible. Jo wanted it to cater both for complete novices who had never been near an oven, and also for more experienced bakers, telling the *Brentwood Gazette*, 'The recipes are achievable by everyone. The response to the book and my blog has been amazing. On Twitter and Facebook, the reactions have been fantastic. I can't describe how wonderful it's been. I pinch myself every day that I'm getting to do this. But the more you get to write about something you like doing, the more you find out and the more doors and avenues open up for you. I pushed myself to come up with different ideas and recipes and really enjoyed doing it. It's given me a whole new purpose; I can experiment, and have a reason to now. It's wonderful to be doing this for a living. I loved compiling it, I loved every moment. It was cathartic; it brought back memories of my childhood, cooking with Nan and the amazing family parties we had. It was such a lovely thing to do.' On top of the success of *A Passion For Baking*, Jo also took another leaf out of Mary's book. She now teaches baking masterclasses from her home in Essex and they quickly became a huge hit with the public, with bookings being taken months in advance.

The popularity of the *Great British Bake Off* had transformed Jo from a stay-at-home mum to a household name ... giving her some of the same opportunities that Mary had. There was no better example of how a popular TV show could make such a marked difference to an individual's life. The show's actual prize might not have been anything substantial, but the rewards afterwards were huge. After the end of series two, TV critic Kevin O'Sullivan noted in his *Sunday Mirror* column: 'More than 5 million cake fans tuned in to the *Great British Bake Off* to see Essex mum Jo win TV's worst-ever trophy. Wooden spoons inside a see-through sphere with some sort of lemon squeezer shoved on the top. Eight weeks of hard kitchen graft ... and this is all she gets! But I guess that's the charm of this innocent slice of Middle England. No big-money prizes, no claptrap about changing lives ... no idiot minor celebs spewing meaningless clichés. Just a good old-fashioned village-hall cooking contest ... Set your ovens to 2012. This is one programme cash-strapped BBC2 won't be axing.'

And Kevin was totally right. *GBBO* was the hit that would just keep growing and growing. Another series was commissioned for 2012. But before then, as with all popular reality TV shows, there would be a couple of spin-offs, in the form of *Junior Bake Off* and the *Great Sport Relief Bake Off*. The first kicked off soon after the second series of *GBBO* had come to an end. Mary and Paul returned to judge a group of young bakers as they went through the same process the adults had done on the main show. The demands, however, were somewhat less daunting for the youngsters.

Rather than elaborate tower cakes and pastries with expensive ingredients, the kids were set challenges of baking far simpler dishes. However, the idea behind the show remained the same and it was screened on the children's TV channel CBBC. Then, in January 2012, celebrities competed on the *Great Sport Relief Bake Off*, to tie in with Sport Relief, the BBC's annual charity fundraising event. The celebrity would-be bakers included TV journalist Anita Rani, actresses Angela Griffin and Sarah Hadland, former *Strictly Come Dancing* judge and choreographer Arlene Phillips, botanist James Wong, garden designer Joe Swift, BBC journalist Fi Glover, *Apprentice* finalist Saira Khan, curator Gus Casely-Hayford, fashion designer Pearl Lowe and weatherman Alex Deakin. Anita Rani eventually won the four-episode mini-series. But Mary wasn't so complimentary about the celebrities' baking skills as a whole. 'They were pretty ropey, although they were lovely,' Mary said in an interview with the *Daily Express* after filming of the series had finished.

By the summer of 2012, preparations were once again in full swing for the return of the *Great British Bake Off*. As in the second series, there were 12 contestants competing across 10 episodes. This time around, filming moved out to the countryside, to picturesque Harptree Court in Somerset. Originally built in 1798, it usually functioned as an award-winning country house open to the public as a high-end bed-and-breakfast retreat. The contestants who would be coming under Mary and Paul's watchful eye included Natasha Stringer, Cathryn Dresser, Peter Maloney, Victoria Chester, Stuart Marston-Smith, Manisha Parmar, Sarah-Jane Willis,

Ryan Chong, Danielle Bryden, Brendan Lynch, James Morton and John Whaite. The series hit screens in August – and by now it had become a staple of British TV.

But while the ratings were better than ever, and fans of the show delighted in its return, the show began to hit the headlines outside of the TV review pages. Unsurprisingly for such a successful show, it had suddenly become newsworthy, too – something that showbiz journalists could latch on to and write about as the series progressed. The coverage wasn't always positive, however, and the show found itself in hot water soon after the third series began.

For instance, it was noted that Smeg fridges featured heavily in the show. Each workstation in the competition kitchen has a fridge emblazoned with a prominent Smeg logo on the front. There would be close-up shots of the fridges as contestants gathered ingredients and prepared to pull together their recipes. To the casual eye, this might not have seemed anything out of the ordinary. However, one viewer complained about it. Andrew Smith, of Manchester, wrote to the *Radio Times* to voice his concerns, saying: 'The Smeg logo was so visible that I counted it 37 times before giving up.' Mr Smith also complained that Smeg's website seemed to indicate a collaboration with the *Great British Bake Off*, as it openly said that it had 'once again teamed up with the show to supply six iconic fridge-freezers'. This might not have been remarkable, were it not for the fact that it meant the BBC's guidelines were in danger of being breached. Any form of product placement is strictly forbidden by the corporation. BBC rules say producers must not feature products for cash or services, and any brands shown must be editorially justified and given limited exposure. The accusation that the BBC was allegedly favouring a brand of fridge and giving it ample coverage in one of its flagship shows was particularly damaging. The BBC was forced to admit that it had breached its own editorial standards in doing so. It admitted to the fact that a loan agreement between Love Productions and the fridge-freezer company 'did not meet editorial guidelines'. It transpired that the Italian firm behind Smeg fridges had loaned the £1,000 appliances at no charge for this series after being approached by staff from the production company. It had also supplied them for the two earlier series. The result was that the BBC asked for the comments on the Smeg website to be removed, and a spokesman for the corporation issued a statement saying: 'It is inevitable that some equipment will be seen in shot but producers are always looking to minimise product prominence. The independent production company had a loan agreement that did not meet editorial guidelines, therefore it is being revised and hire payments will be made.'

That controversy aside, it was Mary who mainly took centre stage when it came to the media coverage. The newspapers couldn't get enough of the doyenne of baking, as the series became ever more popular. And Mary's honesty meant that she also grabbed some major headlines. That was particularly the case when she said, in one interview to publicise the series, that 'young wives' should love cooking – something that flew in the face of feminist ideals that a woman's place in the twenty-first century was most certainly not confined to the kitchen. Modern brides, it is widely believed, should be able to share kitchen duties with their spouse. But Mary was quite vocal and said that she simply did not agree. Her position was that women should accept that they will spend a large proportion of their lives slaving away over a hot stove – and should fully embrace it. The comments were made while she was talking about her daughter Annabel. Mary said: 'She does love cooking. Isn't that lucky for a young wife and mother? You're going to be doing it your whole life, so you might as well enjoy it.' But while many would have agreed with Mary, her comments didn't go down well with some women, who said that it was hard to balance working life with household duties. Some even took to online forums to complain. One said: 'Husbands should be cooking (and cleaning) too! This is 2012!' Another chimed in, saying: 'How about husbands learning to cook?' While Mary's comments may have created a little bit of controversy, it did go to prove that she was principled, and stood by her beliefs – regardless of whether others may have seen them as outdated.

But while she may have seemed outdated on that occasion, there was another moment during the third series where quite the opposite was true ... and Mary became something of a trendsetter. Not only was she the Queen of Baking – suddenly she became the Queen of Fashion, too. Viewers of *GBBO* started noticing Mary's clothes – and went out of their way to remark on how fashionable they were. It became commonplace for her sartorial choices to be discussed on social networking sites such as Twitter, just as much as the cakes that featured on the show. Particularly popular with her fans was a trendy floral bomber jacket from high-street chain Zara. After Mary appeared wearing it on the show, hundreds of comments from fans commenting on how chic and stylish it looked flooded the micro-blogging site. One, calling themselves Incredibly Rich, tweeted: 'Not only is

Mary Berry faultless in the kitchen, that flower print blouse she's wearing is bang on trend. The woman is a goddess.' Rosie Richards commented: 'Yes! Mary Berry is rocking her floral bomber jacket from Zara. Legend.' Jim Taylor added: 'I don't normally tweet about fashion, but Mary Berry looks amazing on *Great British Bake Off* tonight. The "digital floral bomber jacket" is in this autumn.'

At one stage there was such a lot of discussion about the clothes that she was trending on Twitter, with many wondering whether they could still purchase the item. Natalie Longworth said: 'I'm loving Mary Berry's floral bomber jacket. Where can I get one?' But sadly for anyone trying to get their hands on the £29.99 silk jacket, it was unavailable. This prompted Zara to issue a statement on the matter. A spokesman said: 'The jacket was part of last season's spring and summer collection. Unfortunately it is now unavailable.' A similar storm had erupted when Kate Middleton had worn one of Zara's £20 dresses in the days after the Royal Wedding in April 2011. The dress had sold out within days. But because Mary's jacket wasn't available, that wasn't an option. In the days after the show, the floral bomber jacket was being sold on auction site eBay for £200 a piece – more than six times the price it had been in the shops. It was not the first time she had caused a stir with her outfits. The previous week she had worn a hot pink blazer that prompted scores of compliments. One fan said: 'Mary Berry looking serene and wonderful tonight in her pink jacket – ageing gracefully and naturally.' Not only was Mary loved for her baking prowess, but she was becoming a style icon too.

But as usual, the chemistry between Paul and Mary was

what dominated during the course of the third series. Their natural on-screen relationship appeared to grow stronger as the series continued. And off screen they appeared to be forming a genuine friendship too. Paul told how, while driving home from filming on one occasion, he had stopped off at a McDonald's drive-through ... and tried to convince Mary to have a Big Mac. The suggestion didn't go down well with Mary. Paul recounted the incident in an interview with the *Radio Times*: 'I crave salt. We recently filmed our Christmas special and on the way back to our hotel I pulled into a drive-in McDonald's with Bezza – that's my pet name for Mary Berry. I'd been eating cakes all day and had a big craving. [I said:] "Big Mac, large fries ...what do you want, Bezza?" She wasn't impressed.' Mary and Paul's relationship was the glue that held the show together – without it, it was unclear whether the show would have been so successful. And in the third series ratings reached a peak of 6 million – a first for the show in its three-year run. It appeared unstoppable.

As the series progressed, characters were emerging and the tension was increasing as the final drew nearer. Sussex vicar's wife Sarah-Jane became known for regularly crying on the show. Meanwhile, Bristol-based photographer Ryan was repeatedly hitting problems with his baking. Time and again, his bakes ended in disaster, toppling over or disintegrating before the judges' eyes. After he'd had more than his fair share of second chances, he left the competition. One week the hopefuls were even spared an elimination after an on-screen drama halted filming – law student John Whaite sliced open a finger on his right hand while using an electric cake mixer. The accident happened halfway through the episode as the contestants carried out that week's 'showstopper challenge'. John was making a strudel and was seen wearing a blue glove. At first nothing seemed untoward, as John explained: 'I'm having to start again because I stupidly – it's my own fault – I put my finger in the Magimix and just slid it across the blade. It's just knocked me off balance a little but I'll be all right.' But moments later he was seen sitting down as the glove filled with blood and started pouring down his arm. A pale-looking John then said: 'I need to wash it. I keep on feeling dizzy.' Cameras homed in on the 'blood bath', as it was described in the *Daily Mail*, and it was enough to put fans off their scones and clotted cream. One Twitter user said: 'Not expect to see blood on the *Great British Bake Off*. Not hungry any more.' Show co-host Sue Perkins gave a running commentary in her typically laconic style, saying: 'John's been soldiering on with a cut finger, but it's deeper than first feared, and stretching the pastry has stretched the wound. There is a doctor in the marquee. Danny [another contestant] is an intensive care consultant.' John asked to continue, but the cameras followed him as he was led away to get treatment for his injury. And, as he couldn't carry on baking, in the interests of fairness, Mary and Paul decided to call off the elimination and elected to axe two contestants the following week instead. John later returned with his arm in a sling, saying: 'I'm just so gutted because I really think my strudel's going to be amazing.'

However, the incident didn't stop John from progressing to the show's climax. For the first time the show had an all-male final. Alongside John were medical student James and company director Brendan. As the three men battled it out to become Britain's best baker, much was written about the way in which the *Great British Bake Off* had helped to turn baking into a pastime that could be seen as more 'macho'. This was credited in part to Paul's tough-talking criticism – baking had become something that wasn't just a trivial pursuit; it was something that could be taken seriously by men as well as women. As the third series came to a close a report by trade magazine *The Grocer* also found that home baking is on the rise among men across Britain. Again, this was credited to the *Great British Bake Off*, but also to another show on Channel 4, *The Fabulous Baker Brothers*, presented by baker Henry Herbert and his brother Tom. A spokesman for *The Grocer* said: 'When it comes to doing the baking, men are showing an increasing desire to get stuck in – inspired perhaps by male role models such as *The Fabulous Baker Brothers* or Paul Hollywood, artisan baker and presenter of the *Great British Bake Off*.'

And when it came to the final of the third series, Mary and Paul had some tough decisions to make. John was the underdog – and was widely seen as being lucky to have reached that stage of the competition in the first place. James, then 21, was the favourite to walk away with the trophy after being named the 'star baker' of the series three times, and with Mary hailing him for his creativity. Meanwhile Brendan had a wealth of baking experience behind him and had impressed both Mary and Paul with the precise nature of his baking. But, in a shock twist, John was announced as the surprise winner of the series. He couldn't believe his luck ... not least because PR guru Max Clifford said he could easily make £500,000 in the 12 months following his win if he played his cards right and secured similar deals to previous winners Jo Wheatley and Edd

Kimber. John, who had taken up a job on a bank's graduate training scheme, told the *Sun*: 'I'm very lucky to have my job but I definitely want to focus on baking. It would be nice to earn money from the one thing I love doing. So if I can make a career out of baking I will. It just depends how much interest I get now that everyone who watches knows I won. I'm already working on a book and I'd love to do a TV show. I'd be a fool to turn down offers like that, and I don't plan on turning anything down.'

He was the 'surprise' winner because he'd made a series of blunders. As well as dicing his finger, he had put salt into his rum babas instead of sugar and made a torte that looked like a breeze block. But it was his final recipe that seemed to win the competition for him. During the filming process, he had been in the midst of doing his final exams for his law degree at Manchester University. That meant that filming the *Great British Bake Off*, John said, contributed to what he called his 'heaven and hell' of a year, which included the high of the birth of his new nephew. To represent this, he made two different types of chiffon cake, the recipe for which was so elaborate that it ran on to three pages of A4 and included 27 steps. The dark chocolate 'hell' element of the cake was chocolate icing so smooth it appeared like a mirror. Mary couldn't believe what she was seeing, and gasped: 'It is stunning.' Speaking to the *Sun* after being announced as the winner, John said: 'It is a surreal feeling. I wasn't the favourite and had some real disasters. I had a few strong bakes at the beginning but let myself go a bit. When Mel said I'd won, my sister Jane – who normally takes the mickey out of me – was so shocked she almost dropped the baby in her arms.

She was crying and the rest of my family were all jumping up and down.'

And it took John some getting used to being the new flag-bearer for men getting involved in baking … not least because he had been hailed as a heart-throb during the course of the series. 'You'd be amazed how many butch blokes come up to me in the pub and say they can knock up a mean batch of fairy cakes,' he told the *Sun*. 'It did surprise me, because I expected it to be mainly women and kids. But it's good to see that Britain's blokes are baking again. People tend to think that it is only girls that make cakes, so the all-male final was a shock. I hope it does inspire more men to get involved. I've had loads of female and male attention since making the final, which is nice – but I wouldn't say I'm a heart-throb. Most people just want to know why their cakes haven't risen, or ask for tips. I don't mind, though – if it involves food and cakes, I'm listening. It's overwhelming to have so many people saying nice things.'

The final was also considered a triumph because of its record viewing figures. It recorded a peak audience of 6.7 million and an average of 6.1 million – above and beyond anyone's expectations. It even beat shows on all the other main channels, including *Holby City* on BBC1, which peaked at 5.1 million. And as a result there has been speculation that the *Great British Bake Off* could move to BBC1, to accommodate the fact that it is becoming such a big show – something that would send Mary's star rising even further. This was a path well trodden by other shows that had debuted on BBC2 before finding success. *The Apprentice*, fronted by Amstrad tycoon Lord Alan Sugar, was one such example. And speaking at the *Bake Off*, a BBC source was quoted in the *Daily Mirror* in 2012 saying: 'Viewing figures of 6 and 7 million mean a move to the flagship channel has to be looked at. The figures for the final are higher than for the recent series of *Doctor Who* – even Karen Gillan's exit only pulled in 5.9 million.'

Only time will tell if that will happen. But like all shows that have proven a ratings hit in the UK, the people behind *GBBO* saw the potential for taking the show overseas. This has happened to scores of other successful British shows, including *Who Wants To Be A Millionaire?*, *Weakest Link*, *The X Factor*, *Big Brother* and *I'm A Celebrity … Get Me Out Of Here!*. All of those shows have proved to be popular with viewers on our shores before going abroad. And so the same has happened with Mary's show. *Bake Off* is now being shown in Denmark, Sweden, Belgium and Poland, the *Guardian* reported in October 2012, while series of the show were also in the pipeline in Ireland, Norway, France and Australia.

In Sweden the show was called *Hela Sverige Bakar*, which means 'All Sweden is Baking', and it garnered similarly successful ratings. In Mary's place was Sweden's own 'motherly' Birgitta Rasmussen, who had penned her own baking bible, *Sju Sorters Kako* (Seven Kinds of Cake). But while Mary railed against the soggy bottoms, Birgitta's bugbear was the *dödbakade bottnar* ('dead-baked bottoms'). The format remains the same wherever the show is seen, but the menu of bakes that have to be cooked up by the participants is tailored to each country's taste. Cinnamon buns, for example, which are so popular in Sweden that there's a national day dedicated to them, are the show's signature dish there.

Meanwhile, across the border in Denmark, viewers lapped up *Den Store Bagedyst* – or, in English, 'The Great Bake Fight'. The show has smashed all records for factual shows on Danish TV channel DR1. 'This is the closest version to the UK original: if you turned down the sound, you'd never know the difference, though there are subtle pointers, such as more Scandi wood, and no Smeg fridges,' noted Mark Cook in the *Guardian*. The tone of the Danish version is decidedly gothic, too. Mary's equivalent is Neel Rønholt, an excitable blonde woman, while her Paul Hollywood is a slightly older man called Peter Ingemann. Both, however, wear black – perhaps in an attempt to add an element of drama to the proceedings in the same vein as shows like *The X Factor*.

In Belgium the show is called *De Meesterbakker* – or 'The Master Baker' – and it got a withering review from Mark Cook, who said that the set 'really needs a visit from *60 Minute Makeover*. It lacks the jolly aesthetic of the UK version; much of the action seems to happen in a garishly lit warehouse, which means no tent, no flags, and no squirrels with giant testicles.' While with the UK's *Bake Off* the action takes place in marquees, some of the Flemish version is filmed in the would-be bakers' kitchens, leading to 'an awful lot of clutter and mucky sponges you really don't need to see'. Naturally, being filmed in Belgium, the world's chocolate and waffle capital, both make regular appearances – and it follows that the judge is one of the country's best chocolatier-pâtissiers, Bernard Proot.

Down under, in Australia, the *Great Australian Bake Off* has taken off with gusto. The country's own version of *MasterChef* is as big as *The X Factor* is in Britain after being given a dramatic makeover, so it's no surprise that their *Bake*

Off secured a primetime Saturday evening slot. Regular bakes that feature on the menu include national favourites such as lamingtons, a sponge cake covered in chocolate, dipped in coconut and cut into squares.

While with hindsight it is no surprise that the show took off both here and across the globe, head of Love Productions, Richard McKerrow, says it took ages to get it commissioned. 'It took me four years to get it accepted – it was turned down by everyone,' he has said. Unsurprisingly, the next target that McKerrow and his team are eyeing up is the lucrative US market, where they hope they can take the show. 'Now we want to do an American version,' he has said. And after the success of the third series, that looks set to happen. A US network snapped up the rights after seeing the huge cultural impact that the *Great British Bake Off* had in the UK. The network CBS – home to huge TV shows such as *Big Brother*, *Good Morning America* and *CSI: New York* – bought the rights from Love Productions, hoping to replicate its success stateside. McKerrow is expected to oversee the US version of the show, with suggestions indicating that it could simply be called *Bake Off*. But, vitally, this could prove to be a huge moment in Mary's career. It remains to be seen whether, like *The X Factor*'s star judge Simon Cowell, Mary will cross the pond with the show. But there was speculation that CBS did, in fact, want both her and Paul to remain as a duo and front the US version, while continuing to film the UK version. The *Daily Mirror* quoted a US source in 2012 saying: 'They [Mary and Paul] bring that lightness of touch that Americans would love. We are desperate for them to do it – and they're certainly top of the list.' But another insider told the paper that Mary and Paul's busy schedule – which included filming more spin-off shows and an inevitable fourth series – could prove to be a 'stumbling block' for the negotiations. Nevertheless, it appeared that Mary was, understandably, in high demand by TV execs in the US. And if she were signed up, her celebrity would be taken to a whole new level. As all her fans would agree, it would mean even more well-deserved success.

CHAPTER 10

THE QUEEN OF BRITISH BAKING

By 2012, Mary had well and truly established herself as the Queen of British Baking. She had long been a prolific cookery writer, with her books selling millions of copies worldwide. Her journalism on all things baking and home-cooking was widely read by her long-standing fans, as well as people new to cooking for themselves, and Mary had commissions coming out of her ears. She had spread the word about her love of baking with her trusty Aga to thousands through her Aga Workshops at her home in Buckinghamshire and via her popular demonstrations up and down the country. And on top of all that, she had become one of Britain's best-loved TV cooks. At first that had been thanks to her own cookery shows and appearances on daytime TV from *Lorraine* to *The Alan Titchmarsh Show*, which had been lapped up by generations of viewers. But by the summer of 2012, she had transitioned into being a successful reality TV show judge with a third series of the

Great British Bake Off under her belt and more in the pipeline. And despite being in her late seventies, Mary shows no signs of retiring any time soon. Her career is at the peak of its success, some 50 years after it first started. While most people would be winding down their working life, Mary looks like she is happy to keep going and going.

After becoming such a force to be reckoned with in the world of British cookery, it seemed fitting that Mary would get the royal seal of approval too. And that is just what happened. In the Queen's Birthday Honours list 2012, Mary was appointed a Commander of the Order of the British Empire, otherwise known as a CBE. Announced on Saturday 16 June, it was, the Order said, in recognition of her 'services to culinary arts'. Aside from being given a knighthood or made a dame, a CBE is the most senior of all the orders that the Queen can bestow on her subjects. It is more senior to being made an Officer or Member of the British Empire (OBE or MBE).

Mary couldn't believe that she had been honoured in such a prestigious manner, speaking of her delight at being appointed a CBE soon after the news became public. She conducted a TV interview with her local ITV News network soon after it was announced. The interview was carried out in her kitchen at Watercroft, her beloved family home in Buckinghamshire where so much of her good work had been accomplished. Fittingly, Mary sat in front of her trusty light blue Aga as she spoke about how proud both she and her family were that she had been given the honour. She said: 'It's very exciting ... I'm very, very honoured. I've been cooking and writing books and doing a little bit of television for 50 years and recently I've been doing the *Bake Off* which I've really enjoyed because it's got Great Britain baking in schools, in bake-offs, in raising money for the jubilee ... so I feel very honoured.'

Other high-profile figures to be awarded CBEs at the same time as Mary included the Hollywood actress Kate Winslet, star of critically acclaimed films such as *Titanic*, *Revolutionary Road* and *The Reader*, for services to drama. Also awarded were the high-end designer label Mulberry's fashion director Emma Hill, for her services to the British fashion industry, as well as the chief executive and artistic director of the central London performing arts theatre Sadler's Wells, Alistair Spalding, for services to dance. Also decorated on the same day as Mary was the actress and campaigner April Ashley, who received an MBE for services to transgender equality. Born a boy, April became the first Briton to undergo a sex change operation, in Casablanca in 1960. In the media, former *Spectator* editor Alexander Chancellor was awarded a CBE for services to journalism, while alongside Mary in the world of food and drink, Paul Gayler, executive chef at London's prestigious Lanesborough Hotel, was handed an MBE for services to hospitality and charity. Meanwhile, the less well-known but equally deserving people who were awarded honours included Kent farmer Tony Redsell, the UK's largest hop grower, who was awarded an OBE for services to the hops industry.

With such a high pedigree of others being decorated alongside her, Mary couldn't quite believe that she had been chosen. In her typically modest fashion, Mary even questioned whether the CBE was actually meant for her and not another Mary Berry. 'You don't quite know what to say ... Have they made a mistake?' she laughed.

At one point during the course of the interview, Mary read from the letter that had been sent to inform her that she'd been awarded a CBE. Although she had received it some while before it was publicly announced, protocol meant she had to keep it a secret, even from her closest friends and family, until Buckingham Palace revealed the news. The letter was from the clerk to the privy council, Richard Tilbrook. His role as the most senior civil servant in the Privy Council Office, which presents business for the Queen's approval, was to let people know that they had been honoured. While for years Mary had been used to receiving a steady stream of fan mail from her thousands of followers and devotees, she couldn't quite believe that she had been written to by someone so senior in the British establishment, and on such an important matter. Reading from the letter, Mary said: 'And then it all goes on very formally and at the end it says: "I am, madam, your obedient servant Richard Tilbrook", and nobody ever writes to me as an obedient servant, so it's very, very exciting.'

Even for Mary, who has achieved so much in her life and career, receiving a CBE was a pivotal moment. Mary took a moment to reflect on what her parents, Margaret and Alleyne, would have thought of it. Understandably, she sounded emotional as she spoke of how proud they would have been to see their daughter come from her cookery classes at Bath High School, where by her own admission she had struggled to get even the most basic qualifications, to receiving one of the highest honours the Queen can bestow on her subjects. Her parents were inevitably at the forefront of Mary's mind as she and her close family, including Paul and her two children Tom and Annabel, raised their glasses to toast the day she received her gong.

Mary said: 'My parents are no longer in this world but it's the sort of thing you immediately want to ring your parents [about]. But you're not allowed to – it's in strict confidence. Looking back on all the years that I've been cooking, this sort of thing would never have entered into my head ... I'm really chuffed. I've been waiting for the 16th for a long time, and I can tell you there will be a few bottles opened and the children will be very thrilled – my children. It'll be a very, very happy day.'

On the day itself Mary was invited to attend Buckingham Palace with her family, receiving the medal representing her CBE from Prince Charles, to whom it usually falls to present all honours other than knighthoods and damehoods, which are presented in formal ceremonies by the Queen. Following that, there was a photo call in the grounds of the palace followed by a drinks reception. In short, it was a spectacular day, and a fitting way to mark all the successes of Mary's brilliant career.

It is during the course of that spectacular career that Mary has often been called a trailblazer, a pioneer and the first of a kind when it comes to her cookery. The awarding of the CBE seems to confirm this. Long before Nigella Lawson, Jamie Oliver, Gordon Ramsay et al, Mary set the standard very high for other celebrity cooks. While Jamie has been honoured with an MBE for his contribution to changing the way school dinners are served across the UK, no other celebrity cook in the UK has been honoured with a CBE, apart from Mary's contemporary Delia Smith.

But it appeared that 2012 really was the year when Mary was to be formally recognised as the true doyenne of her craft. Soon after receiving her CBE, in July 2012, she was given an honorary degree for her lifelong achievements in her field back where it all began – in Bath. Some 50 years after she left the spa town for the bright lights of London to try to break into the world of cookery, she was welcomed back there as the ultimate successful cook and was given an honorary degree by Bath Spa University. Fittingly, the university incorporates the former Bath College of Domestic Science where Mary had studied as a teenager after leaving Bath High School. Although Mary had never got a degree as a youngster herself, it seemed she had come full circle, receiving the ultimate honour from the place where she had first discovered her love of cooking. While for years her fans had given Mary all the recognition she needed, it was undeniably nice for her to receive such formal recognition in the form of her CBE and honorary degree. After receiving the degree, Mary told a reporter from the *Bath Chronicle*: 'I am immensely honoured to be here. When I got the letter saying I was being given an honorary degree I couldn't believe it. It is lovely that I am able to be a part of the students' big day.' Mary also referred to the special place Bath held in her heart and how she would always love the city, not least because it was the place she grew up and where her parents had played such an integral part in civic life. Mary said: 'It has changed since I was a child; the buildings are cleaner and there is so much to offer both tourists and residents. The university is set in beautiful surroundings and it must be lovely to study here.' Alongside Mary were other notable figures receiving honorary degrees at the Newton Park campus, including shoe designer Manolo Blahnik, Golden-Oldies charity founder Grenville Jones, journalism professor Ian Hargreaves and technology author Miller

Puckette. They received their degrees alongside hundreds of normal undergraduate students. The part that Mary and the others had played in developing their fields was acknowledged at the event by the university's vice-chancellor, Professor Christina Slade, who presented the degrees. She said: 'At Bath Spa University we foster an ethos of creativity, culture and enterprise, and we want our students to become global citizens, ready to make a difference. There can be no better inspiration for them than these internationally respected figures.'

Time and time again, the ease with which Mary took to the job of being a cook in the public eye and also the simplicity of her recipes appears to have been what has set her apart from those who have followed her. She told the *Daily Telegraph* that anyone can create a wholesome meal that's a joy to eat, even on a small budget: 'Home-cooked food doesn't have to be expensive. Pick a simple but delicious dish such as my shepherd's pie with cheese-topped potatoes. Tiny bunches of flowers or foliage from the garden and tea lights on the table make an immediately impressive look.' Reflecting on why she received her CBE, Mary acknowledged how successful this approach had been. Creating simple recipes that worked time and time again had always been her aim. If people could cook her recipes, that was all she wanted. She said: 'I always enjoyed the teaching ... I started off teaching and then you do a bit over the radio, *Woman's Hour* and things like that. And then a little bit of television. It's just like a big cookery class. And then when you write books, I like to give that extra little detail. And people seem to enjoy that ... where you can go wrong, and we really test all the recipes so that when people make them they work. I think if you ask anybody, I think they would say: "I do her recipes because they work."'

The practicality of Mary's recipes is what has set her apart from the crowd – and it's something she's always emphasised when speaking about her work over the years. In one of Mary's books she says that it's important to 'be methodical and follow the recipe meticulously'. It seems that there is no room for creativity by the baker, if they want to make sure that they get the perfect outcome. During her *Desert Island Discs* interview, Kirsty Young asked whether Mary's insistence that the recipe is followed to the letter was an indicator that she was 'bossy'. Mary, it seemed, was afraid of being branded as such and replied: 'I am quite bossy in the kitchen, just to see that everything runs smoothly. I hope I'm not bossy, I'm just giving advice to get the best results.'

But in a roundabout way it shows that Mary's books were always precise and detailed, as Mary tried to make cooking and baking as easy as possible for her readers. Mary's approach in the kitchen reflects her calm demeanour. Other chefs, such as Jamie Oliver, have advocated different approaches in the kitchen. Some of Jamie's recipes advocate using a 'handful' of onion or 'a sprinkling' of garlic, for instance. But it's not an approach that Mary has ever taken. 'I mean the whole thing is to give it time and not do it in a rush for the first time,' she told *Desert Island Discs*. 'And follow the recipe carefully. And with baking you do have to weigh the ingredients. So often people say, well my gran was a great cook but she never weighed anything. But that gran often had a handle-less cup and a particular spoon and a small selection of things that she baked. And so they put three cups of that, two spoons of that, and it did work every time.'

Over the years Mary has dispensed simple tips that she has used in the kitchen to make her recipes successful. And while Mary has always maintained a slim frame herself, and been the epitome of health by regularly playing tennis, working in her garden and restricting herself to just a small slice of cake when testing the recipes on *GBBO*, she's never been one to shy away from using full-fat ingredients in her cooking. If you want your cake to rise properly or the dish to come out right, 'healthy' alternatives just won't do. 'Use the right fat,' she wrote in the *Sunday Telegraph*. 'If you use margarine or butter, it must be really soft and squishy, and ready to be beaten straight away. Do not use a low-fat one, as [the] results will be disastrous. Soft butter or a spread from the fridge is fine, as long as you are using an electric beater.' And she had a similar principle when it comes to using icing and chocolate. 'Most cakes are best iced after freezing, unless they are filled with buttercream,' she wrote. 'Use the right chocolate. I like Bournville as the cocoa solids content isn't too high (39 per cent – any more and it can separate). It has an excellent flavour, and is good value.' Mary also advocates using ready-made filo pastry.

Another of Mary's favourite tips is not to use extra baking powder when making a cake as, she says, it will cause it to 'rise up and then fall down'. Second only to the soggy bottom, a collapsed cake, it would seem, is a major faux pas in Mary's world. But even Mary admits she could fall foul of one of her own recipes, such as her signature dish, the Victoria sponge, going wrong. She told the *Daily Express*: 'I do have disasters from time to time because you go out in the garden and forget the thing!' That makes us all feel a bit better. 'Mary Berry's Victoria sponge could sink if I opened the door, or used the wrong fat or something, because I mean I could almost do it in the dark, but I do measure very carefully and I make sure I use the right ingredients,' she told *Desert Island Discs*. 'Over-baking gives a dry result. Watch it in the oven during the last stage of cooking. It should be shrinking away from the side of the tin. When you press your finger in the middle, the mixture should spring back. When you've made a cake, put your own notes on the recipe such as "In my oven it took five minutes less" or "This cake freezes well".'

Correct kitchen equipment has always been important in preventing a total cake collapse, Mary says. 'Use the right type of tin. For a Victoria sponge, if it isn't in a 20cm (8in) tin it will not be as spongy – it will be thinner, it will cook quicker and won't rise as well,' Mary wrote. Other 'kitchenalia', as she calls it, comes in handy too. 'My secret brilliant tool: a small hand-mixer,' she wrote. 'It doesn't take up much room and saves so much time. You can buy one from about £12.' The products that she uses in the kitchen are half the fun of baking for Mary. Over the years she's become a big collector of kitchenware, just as she's become a keen recipe writer. 'I've always collected vintage kitchenalia because it's beautifully made and I love to see things that have been used down the ages,' she told the *Daily Telegraph*. 'I used to display my collection over the Aga, but a kitchen gets very dirty so I had it framed instead. You'll see everything from vegetable and herb choppers to whisks, sugar snippers and bottle openers. One of my favourite items is a nineteenth-century tin opener used to open cans of bully beef. It has a bull's head with a spike on top. I also have a breadboard carved with the words, "Give us this day our daily bread". I've been in and out of junk shops all my married life. It's my relaxation.' But equally, Mary says she's cautious about modern gadgetry, which is often expensive but ultimately quite useless. 'There is such a wide array of kitchen gadgetry available and although a lot of it looks pretty not all of it is particularly useful,' she said. 'I could never imagine finding much use for an onion chopper, for instance. However a good set of digital scales tends to make baking a lot easier. Until a couple of years ago I always used traditional scales with weights. Now I have a wonderful set of Escali digital scales and they do tend to be more accurate, especially when you are using very small amounts of spice or seasoning.' For Mary the most useful items are those that have no bells and whistles. In particular, Mary says, she relies on a sharp knife to get her through most of her cooking tasks. 'The thing I use more than anything else is a knife; a jolly sharp Victorinox,' she told the *Independent*. 'I'm often to be found sharpening them myself with my Chantry sharpener, which does a very good job … The thing I use least? An ice-cream machine. I've had several of them over the years, but with my latest recipe you make a meringue mix and add things straight to that, rather than remixing it in a machine. So I've made my own piece of kit redundant.' While Mary has certainly proven herself able to move with the times and reinvent herself from a cook into a reality TV judge, mod cons in the kitchen don't always seem to do it for her.

As someone who is so excellent at cooking, it is no wonder that Mary loves to entertain with dinner parties. She has spoken at length about how she loves nothing more than to have close friends and family over for home-cooked meals at Watercroft. Company, especially around the dining table, is something Mary seems to thrive on. And for Mary, when it comes to large gatherings – especially family gatherings – it's important to make sure everyone takes part in the preparation process. 'For big gatherings, the trick is to give guests something to do,' she told the *Daily Telegraph* in 2001. 'My mother, who is 95, enjoys peeling sprouts,' she says. 'Sarah, my daughter-in-law, will peel grapes meticulously for fruit salad. And my daughter Annabel is wonderful at curry.' Having family over for meals and making time to all sit down together is something that Mary still thinks should be a vitally important part of our day-to-day lives. While life becomes busier – not least for Mary – she still thinks it's essential to clear space to bond with loved ones and spend time together. 'My family is what I cherish most in life and over the years I've made sure that we've cemented our relationships round the dinner table,' she said in a 2007 interview with the *Scotsman*. 'Now my children are grown up and I have four grandchildren I still often welcome them home and make sure we get together to eat. I've always encouraged family meals round the table. My mother is 102 years old and my grandchildren are all under five but it is amazing how, when people are content and sitting having a good meal, tongues fly and you learn more about their lives.' Mary is a great believer in food having the power to unite people – not only through learning how to cook it, but by enjoying it together too.

With such an encyclopaedic knowledge of good food and being a judge on the *Great British Bake Off*, one might imagine that when it came to eating other people's food, Mary might be quite snobbish. It would be easy to assume that she would only eat at the finest restaurants in the West End of London. However, it appears that couldn't be further from the truth. Mary has long been a keen promoter of keeping food simple, but tasty. When asked, in an interview with the *Independent,* where she would dine out if she only had £10 to spend, she insisted she would pick a popular chain restaurant. 'I'd go where I usually take my grandchildren: Pizza Express,' she said. 'They do very good food for comparatively little money. Their pizzas are really quite good and it's all very efficient and comfortable.' And it seems that, even when she does have a little more money to spend on dining out, Mary chooses not to pick lavish places, but rather a few old haunts that she and Paul frequent regularly in and around their home village. 'We don't get up to town that much, so I'm no connoisseur of posh London food,' Mary told the *Independent.* Seasonal food and a warm welcome count for more than the latest fancy food trend or cutting-edge interior design. The bubble and squeak with egg, bacon and hollandaise sauce at the Old Queen's Head in Penn is one of her favourites. 'Near us in Penn, High Wycombe, there's a lovely pub that does lots of traditional food like hotpot and slowroasted pork; I enjoy that sort of relaxed pub eating, so I'd say that's my favourite.' But like any foodie, Mary occasionally treats herself to eating out at high-end restaurants, telling the BBC: 'Le Manoir aux Quat'Saisons is a huge treat: Raymond Blanc makes you feel very special ... We spend a lot of time in Salcombe in Devon, and there's a place there called the South Sands Hotel. It's overlooking the sea, with windows down to the floor so you feel like you could jump in. It has a wonderful fish menu created by Mitch Tonks.'

But even when she's not dining out, Mary prefers to keep her food simple. In recent years Heston Blumenthal has risen to fame for his hugely inventive and off-the-wall dishes. They have included wacky concepts such as snail porridge and bacon ice cream. The creation process of these dishes, Heston has said, is more like being a scientist experimenting in a laboratory, rather than being a cook. His creations have propelled him to stardom as a TV chef, fronting a host of programmes including one in which he replicated the feasting traditions of bygone eras. In one episode he attempted to recreate a Cockentrice, which in Tudor times was seen as a mythical beast to be eaten during huge feasts, which was really made by sewing different animals together. Heston revealed that Henry VIII apparently held a feast for Francis I of France during which a Cockentrice was served, made out of the front half of a pig sewn to the back half of a chicken. But Heston, ever the experimentalist when it comes to cooking, decided to include a lamb and a goose as well. Meanwhile, Heston's restaurant, The Fat Duck in Bray, Berkshire, where he serves many of his most eccentric and sought-after dishes to the public in the form of lavish tasting menus, has a long waiting list; you must book months in advance to secure a table. But while Heston's brand of creativity in cookery has become fashionable in restaurant years, Mary's tastes have remained far simpler. She has always maintained that taste and enjoyment of food should come before trends and modern fashions in cookery. Comfort food should be embraced wholeheartedly, and this is something that Mary has referred to in interviews over the years. Just because it's simple, doesn't mean it's any less worthwhile. 'I really like boiled eggs or toast and marmalade,' she told the *Independent*. 'I've made loads of marmalade this year, so I'd have that. I save all my clementine and satsuma peelings and put them in the freezer and use them to bulk out my preserve – it gives it its own identity. If I have a choice of bread to have it on I always like Paul Hollywood's seeded variety.' And if, hypothetically, she were to become a castaway on a desert island, and faced the prospect of having one of her final meals, she insists it would still be kept simple. 'It would be a simple pasta recipe,' she told the *Independent*. 'First boil some pasta in salted water. Then cook some broccoli or, if in season, asparagus. Now take dry cured ham, snip it into chunks and fry in a pan. Add some cream (it has to be proper dairy) and mix it all together. Drain your pasta, then add the sauce. I could live off that for quite a while.'

In fact, this idea of becoming a desert-island castaway was a notion Mary would return to in 2012, soon after she was presented with her CBE and honorary degree. She was invited to take part in the long-running Radio 4 programme *Desert Island Discs*. The show has a long, rich history. First broadcast on 29 January 1942, it was devised and originally presented by the legendary English radio broadcaster Roy Plomley. Since then the show has run and run, leaving it holding the record for the longest-running factual programme in the history of radio. On top of that, it has also become one of the longest-running programmes in worldwide radio history. The format has remained the same throughout, too. One guest appears on the show per episode. During the course of that episode, they will choose eight pieces of music, recordings of which they would take with them if they were to go and stay on a deserted island. As well as their music, the 'castaways', as they are referred to on the show, are permitted to take one book and one luxury item away with them on their imaginary trip. To tie in with the theme of the show, its theme tune is *By the Sleepy Lagoon*, which was composed by Eric Coates in 1930. This has remained the same since the show was first broadcast in the 1940s. Since 2006 the show has been presented by the former newsreader Kirsty Young, who guides the guests through their musical choices, interspersing them with chats about key moments in their life. Over the years a huge array of high-profile stars from the world of film, music, politics and TV has appeared in the show's hot seat, including, in recent years, the deputy prime minister and leader of the Liberal Democrats Nick Clegg, broadcaster and naturalist Sir David Attenborough, novelist Vikram Seth, *Strictly Come Dancing* head judge Len Goodman, the comedian Michael McIntyre and the Hollywood actress Goldie Hawn.

So it was an honour in itself for Mary to be asked on to the show. The songs she chose give a further insight into her personality and exactly what makes her tick, both inside and outside of the kitchen. The first piece of music was by Dame Gracie Field, called 'Wish Me Luck As You Wave Me Goodbye'. It became popular during the Second World War, when Mary was growing up in Bath, and the song itself went on to have patriotic resonances in films such as 1939's *Shipyard Sally*. It was later re-recorded by the forces' sweetheart, Vera Lynn, as well as Elsie Carlisle. For Mary, it brought back memories of growing up during the war, but also, more poignantly, of her mother Margaret, who loved the song. At the time of recording *Desert Island Discs,* Margaret had recently passed away – and so the choice had extra meaning for Mary. 'I can so remember after the war and the end of the war, her singing "Wish Me Luck As You Wave Me Goodbye,"' Mary said. 'And my mother, who died quite recently at 105; my brothers very kindly let me do the service. And I was thinking, now what shall we end up with? And it suddenly crossed my mind; of course, Mum absolutely loved that. I've chosen a nice noisy version.'

Mary's second piece of music was 'Spring' from Vivaldi's 'The Four Seasons', a set of four violin concertos by the Italian composer. Composed in 1723, 'The Four Seasons' is Vivaldi's best-known work, and is among the most popular pieces of Baroque music. The texture of each concerto is varied, each resembling its respective season. So 'Winter' is peppered with silvery pizzicato notes from the high strings, calling to mind icy rain, whereas 'Summer' evokes a thunderstorm in its final movement, which is why the movement is often dubbed 'Storm'. 'Spring', meanwhile, is more upbeat and staccato at times, representing, some say, the beginnings of new life. In short, the piece reminded Mary of her favourite time of year – when her garden at Watercroft, which she and Paul spend many a happy hour tending to, would be coming in to bloom. Explaining the choice, Mary said: 'I love it, it is mellow, and being Spring, it is my favourite season. I think when you look in the garden, after about March, it is full of promise. Things are coming up, and with that in the background would be lovely.'

For her next piece, Mary went for a change of tack, opting for Sir Cliff Richard's 'Summer Holiday'. This upbeat song has become a legendary UK track as the theme song of the 1963 film of the same name, which became the second most popular film at the British box office in the year that it was released. It was, at the time, considered a 'breakthrough musical', in part because of the way dance was – for the first time – used as well as singing. The song 'Summer Holiday' reached number one in the UK charts, as did other tracks from the film's soundtrack, including 'The Next Time', 'Bachelor Boy' and 'Foot Tapper'. But for Mary, the theme song simply reminded her of some of the happiest times in her life – when she went on holiday with her family. 'We always used to have holidays with our three children. We would go every year to Devon,' Mary said. 'And Dad had a VW camper van which he lent to my two brothers and to me and we all loved it. And on the way down we would be playing "Summer Holiday" and Cliff Richard as we went along, and everybody was thinking well, we are going to get there.'

Her fourth piece was a track recorded by Susan Boyle. Scottish-born Susan became an unlikely star in 2009; her performance on the ITV1 reality show *Britain's Got Talent* of *Les Misérables* track 'I Dreamed A Dream' became a worldwide phenomenon. Videos of the audition garnered more than 100 million hits on the video-sharing website YouTube alone. But beyond that, after coming second on that year's series of *BGT*, she went on to record an album, which shot to number one around the globe, including in the tough-to-crack US market. Aside from her breathtaking vocals, it was Susan's back story that appeared to win the hearts of people around the globe. She had been left heartbroken after her mother, who had been her closest friend, had died in the years prior to her audition. 'I was very lost, and very lonely,' said Susan. She lived in a council house in the small Scottish village of Blackburn, where she had been bullied by local youths who cruelly branded her 'Simple Susan'. But her life had completely turned around and changed forever after her appearance on reality TV. Mary couldn't help but be swept away by her story and picked her recording of 'How Great Thou Art' from Susan's debut album. 'I am a huge admirer,' Mary said on the show. 'I think she has done so magnificently, and what a voice ... and I know she worked very hard to get there.'

Her next piece of music was 'Onward, Christian Soldiers', a nineteenth-century English hymn. The words of the hymn were written more recently by Sabine Baring-Gould in 1985, while the music itself had been composed by Arthur Sullivan in 1871. He called the tune 'St Gertrude' after the wife of his friend Ernest Clay Ker Seymer, who owned the country house where Sullivan composed it. And it was part of this history of the hymn that first attracted Mary to the piece of music and made her aware of it. Arthur Sullivan regularly visited Watercroft, where Sir George Grove lived. He composed the piece of music in the summerhouse at Watercroft, years before Mary and Paul came to own it. After becoming aware of the hymn's links to their home, Mary and Paul would often play the track, and it became a favourite of theirs over the years. On top of that, it came to have a rich personal history, because it was played at their son Tom's wedding. 'We had it at Tom and Sarah's wedding, and we loved it,' Mary revealed in her interview. Her daughter Annabel's future husband Dan, however, wasn't so keen. 'Then when Annabel and Dan got married, Dan quite firmly said, "I am not going to march down the aisle with

Annabel to war."' Her next song, however, was a reminder of Annabel's wedding. Mary picked 'Lord of the Dance', another hymn with words written by English songwriter Sydney Carter in 1967. It was a big feature of Annabel's big day. 'This reminds me so much of Annabel's wedding,' said Mary. 'We were lucky enough to have sun and lots of jollity and lots of singing and dancing. A great day.'

Mary appeared to be picking songs that reminded her of her family – and reminded her of her close bond with her family. It was no coincidence, then, that one of the songs she picked was dedicated to William. The British rocker Rod Stewart's track 'Sailing' was her next choice. The song had originally been released in 1972 by the Sutherland Brothers, and then Rod re-recorded it. When he released it three years later, it became a UK number one hit, staying at the top of the charts for a total of four weeks. And it was around then that Mary's sons William and Tom became fans of it. Like typical youngsters, they would have the track blaring out of their bedrooms – and inevitably, when Mary hears the track even today, it reminds her of their childhood. 'It was something that the boys, when they were back from school, they would have it on full blast upstairs,' said Mary. 'When Will's funeral came, not only did we have "Onward Christian Soldiers" but we finished with "Sailing", to remember him.' Put in this context, it is understandable why Mary would pick the song as her choice if she had to take just one with her to the hypothetical desert island. She added: 'The one that I would take, I think to remind me of William, would be Rod Stewart singing "Sailing".'

Mary's final choice was slightly more upbeat. It was the hugely popular Swedish group Abba's huge track 'Mamma

Mia', which became a chart-topper when it was released in 1975. It would also go on to be the title of a musical inspired by the music of Abba. *Mamma Mia!* tells the story of a woman living on a Greek island, whose daughter is planning to get married. The mother has no clue who the father is … but three of her ex-boyfriends, each of whom could be her daughter's dad, have been invited to the big day. Abba's oeuvre is interspersed throughout the story as it all unravels. Over 42 million people have seen the stage show, which has grossed $2 billion worldwide since its 1999 debut. A film adaptation starring Meryl Streep, Colin Firth, Pierce Brosnan and Amanda Seyfried was released in July 2008 and was a huge box-office hit worldwide. The film, Mary says, was one of her favourites – and the reason she decided to pick the song as her eighth and final choice on *Desert Island Discs*. 'My husband and a group of chaps, I think it's about once in six weeks, they play cards,' explained Mary. 'And of course all the wives, off we go to a cinema, or we might even come to London, some treat, local pub … but we all went to *Mamma Mia!* and it was hilarious. And you sit in the seats and you look round and you see all groups of girls, perhaps I shouldn't call myself a girl, all in groups and I think everybody who went to see that in the cinema thoroughly enjoyed it. You come out singing.'

When it came to picking the book that she would take with her, Mary's combined love of gardening and cooking was made clear. 'I would like to take with me a book that I have in the kitchen, because I have gardening books in the kitchen, the *[RHS] A–Z Encyclopedia of Garden Plants*. It is a huge book and it has a photograph of every single plant. I may find some plants there. And also I am not staying on that island too long, I am going to be rescued, so I want to go on planning the garden.' Meanwhile, her luxury item was a cashmere rug. 'Everybody would say I am the coldest mortal in the world, [so] I think I would have a huge, cashmere, beautiful rug,' she said. 'I know it is going to be cold at nights there, and the thought of being on that sand with nothing round me, no loving children or husband, I'll have that rug to keep me warm. Pure cashmere, please.'

Of course, the truth is there's very little chance of Mary disappearing – metaphorically or otherwise – any time soon. She is now, more than ever, a huge part of mainstream British culture, both in the kitchen and on TV. Mary appears to have achieved it all. She has a glittering career that appears to be going from strength to strength, and no chance of slowing down any time soon. On top of that, she has the most idyllic family life, with her loyal husband Paul, her children and her grandchildren. Of course, it has been tinged with the tragedy of William's death. But Mary sees life as a learning curve. She has learnt from William's death about the importance of family and has helped others through similarly difficult, gut-wrenching situations with her charity work. Most of all, she has helped others on their own learning curve in the kitchen, through her books, TV shows and workshops. And she intends to carry on doing all of this for a long time yet.

Retirement, Mary insists, is simply not an option. 'I don't even think of it as a job, it's just something I love to do,' she told the *Daily Mail*. When asked on *Desert Island Discs* whether, like others her age, she and Paul would consider taking time off from her busy schedule and disappearing on a seven-week cruise, she laughed off the suggestion. 'The seven-week cruise wouldn't be on,' Mary said. 'I think he

[Paul] would take me to see some golf matches or something. I love my husband dearly and he supports me in every way. When I came back from the *Bake Off* last night there was a glass of Sauvignon Blanc in his hand, just like my father with his gin and tonic, and together we have supper.' And when it came to the R-word – retirement – Mary seemed dumbfounded by the suggestion. It's a word that, quite simply, is not in her vocabulary. 'Retiring? Why would I retire? I am so blessed with good health, I love what I do, and I am very honoured to be asked to still be in the *Bake Off*,' she told *Desert Island Discs*. 'I love it.' Her devotees – whether they first discovered her with the release of the *Hamlyn All Colour Cook Book* or more recently on the *Great British Bake Off* – will collectively breathe a sigh of relief after hearing that.

Given everything she's achieved, you wouldn't be surprised to see Mary's life given the movie treatment, and if any producer needs tips on whom to cast, then Mary has it clear in her mind who would play her. 'The lovely Dame Judi Dench,' she told the *Scotsman*. While Mary loves cookery, it seems her fans love her too. And will continue to do so for a long time yet. What would they do without her? After all, Mary Berry truly is the Queen of British Baking.